1

STATE TAXATION OF PERSONAL INCOMES

STUDIES IN HISTORY, ECONOMICS AND PUBLIC LAW

EDITED BY THE FACULTY OF POLITICAL SCIENCE
OF COLUMBIA UNIVERSITY

Volume CI]   [Number 1

Whole Number 229

STATE TAXATION OF PERSONAL INCOMES

BY

ALZADA COMSTOCK

AMS PRESS
NEW YORK

COLUMBIA UNIVERSITY
STUDIES IN THE
SOCIAL SCIENCES

229

The Series was formerly known as
Studies in History, Economics and Public Law.

Reprinted with the permission of Columbia University Press
From the edition of 1921, New York
First AMS EDITION published 1969
Manufactured in the United States of America

Library of Congress Catalogue Card Number: 74-78007

AMS PRESS, INC.
NEW YORK, N. Y. 10003

PREFACE

BELIEVING that the fiscal aspects of state income taxes were in danger of being overlooked in the enthusiasm for progressive income taxation, the writer made a brief study of the yield and cost of these taxes early in 1920. The paper appeared as " Fiscal Aspects of State Income Taxes " in the *American Economic Review* for June, 1920. In the present study an attempt has been made to present more fully the facts which represent the financial standing of these taxes, together with a description of their background and of the manner in which they operate.

The writer wishes to acknowledge indebtedness to Mr. A. E. Holcomb of the National Tax Association for helpful suggestions and for permission to reprint the material in the appendices, to Mr. Nils P. Haugen, formerly chairman of the Wisconsin Tax Commission and to other state officials who have generously supplied information which was not available in published reports, and especially to Professor Edwin R. A. Seligman of Columbia University, under whose direction the study was carried on and whose constructive criticism made its accomplishment possible.

ALZADA COMSTOCK

MOUNT HOLYOKE COLLEGE, JUNE 20, 1921.

TABLE OF CONTENTS

APPENDIX I

APPENDIX II

CHAPTER I

THE EVOLUTION OF THE STATE INCOME TAX

IN the second decade of the twentieth century personal incomes became an important source of public revenue With the extraordinary demands upon government treasuries during the period of the European War and the enlarged financial needs in time of peace it became necessary to reach sources which were almost untouched before the present era of great expenditures. In modern industrial countries, in which the majority of incomes are in the form of money and instruments of credit, such resources may be found and utilized easily and quickly. The productivity and elasticity of taxes on individual incomes made possible the extension of existing systems of income taxation as well as successful experiments with new income taxes.

In the United States the state governments as well as the federal took advantage of the elasticity of income taxes in revising their tax systems to meet the changing needs of this period. The result, from a critical and historical point of view, is an aggregation of examples of possible income tax methods rather than the development of an American income tax policy, for no two state income taxes are alike, even in their essentials. Moreover, many of the precedents of method and of administrative devices have been drawn from European countries instead of the American experience of nearly three centuries of colonial and state taxation. In spite of the tendency of the states to abandon the older legislation and to ignore its lessons, both constructive and negative, the influences of the traditional tax systems persist, playing an almost unrecognized part in shaping the revenue systems of today. The obvious and contemporary explanations of the present period of income tax development are satisfying only when they are illuminated by the long history of the successes and failures of the attempts of the states to tax income and property.

1. *Early faculty taxes* [1]

The earliest examples of taxes which may be said to be the forerunners of the state income taxes of today are the " ability " or " faculty " taxes used in the American colonies. The first reference to taxpaying ability appears in an act passed in the Massachusetts Bay Colony in 1634, providing for the assessment of each resident " according to his estate and with consideration of all other his abilityes whatsoever," but this provision appears to have been interpreted as applying to property only. Seven years later, in New Plymouth, " faculties and personal abilities " were distinguished from visible property for the purposes of taxation, a distinction which was apparently maintained in the actual assessment of the taxes. In 1646 a definition of faculty appeared for the first time, in the order of the Massachusetts Bay Company that artisans and tradesmen should be assessed for their "returns and gains " in the same proportion as property-holders were assessed for " the produce of their estates." From this time forward the principle of taxation according to faculty made steady headway in the New

---

[1] The principal sources of information used in summarizing the history of income taxes up to 1900 are Edwin R. A. Seligman, *The Income Tax* (Revised ed., New York, 1914), and Delos O. Kinsman, *The Income Tax in the Commonwealths of the United States* (New York, 1903).

England colonies. Connecticut followed in 1650, Rhode Island in 1673, New Hampshire in 1719, and Vermont in 1788. In Rhode Island alone the tax dropped out of existence before the outbreak of the Revolution. In Massachusetts, on the other hand, the faculty taxes were utilized during the Revolution for the purpose of reaching war profits as well as ordinary income.

Outside of New England the growth of faculty taxes was slower. In New York the tax failed to appear at all. The first indication of an attempt in the middle or southern colonies to apportion taxes according to faculty came in New Jersey in 1684, nearly half a century after the beginning in New England. In the course of the eighteenth century five other colonies, Pennsylvania, Delaware, Maryland, Virginia, and South Carolina, undertook taxation according to income or profits. Few of these taxes survived the economic changes of the early national era. The only tax which continued with an unbroken record down to the modern period was that of Massachusetts, which gave way to a new income tax in 1916.

Although the early statutes contain many references to " income," the colonial faculty taxes are not to be confused with the income taxes of the present day. The colonial taxes were rarely based on income actually received, but represented assessments of certain fixed amounts which were determined in most instances by the nature of the taxpayer's employment. For this reason the faculty taxes soon came to bear little relation to the earnings of the person assessed, and to become unequal and unjust in their burden. As taxes on property developed the faculty taxes appeared increasingly arbitrary, and they tended to give place to income taxes or to drop out of existence.

2. *State income taxes in the nineteenth century*

The financial troubles of 1837 and the following years brought about a fresh development in the taxation of incomes. It was not long before the effects of the great crisis made themseves felt in the revenues of the states, which soon set about the business of increasing their tax receipts. As a result the country entered upon a second phase of the state taxation of incomes, in which the taxes were levied upon income actually received instead of upon the assumed income or profits of certain classes of taxpayers. New England, which was less seriously affected by the financial disturbances of the time, had no share in the new income tax movement, but six middle and southern states, Pennsylvania, Maryland, Virginia, North Carolina. Florida, and Alabama, tried to raise funds through income taxes at this time.

If the Civil War had not brought new financial emergencies, particularly in the affairs of the southern states, the income taxes adopted during the forties would probably have been abandoned. Only six, the faculty taxes of Massachusetts and South Carolina, and the newer income taxes of Pennsylvania, Virginia, North Carolina, and Alabama, were in existence when the war broke out.

In the years of the war and the following period of reconstruction the states turned again to the income tax as a means of relief and a source of additional revenue in a time of great financial need. The tax was developed almost wholly in the southern states, where the demand for funds was most pressing. The Massachusetts and Pennsylvania laws were undisturbed. Four of the southern states, Virginia, North Carolina, South Carolina, and Alabama, made use of the income tax systems already in existence for the production of additional revenue. Several other states were induced to make the experiment. Georgia, Missouri,

Texas, Louisiana, West Virginia, and Kentucky tried income taxes in various forms, but all of the taxes soon disappeared with the exception of that of Louisiana, which was continued with negligible success until the end of the century. Meanwhile the northern states, which, in spite of their heavy burden, were in far less serious straits, neglected the tax. State income taxes seemed to bear the marks of a last resort for an over-burdened government.

The lowest ebb in the history of state income taxes was reached in the period 1884 to 1897. The only income taxes in force during this time were those of Massachusetts, Virginia, North Carolina, and Louisiana. In Massachusetts and Louisiana the assessment of personal incomes had almost disappeared, and in Virginia and North Carolina the yield was extremely small. In fact, the whole history of state income taxes from the close of the Civil War to the introduction of a new plan of taxation by Wisconsin in 1911 is almost entirely a record of failure. With almost no exceptions the administration of the laws was poor, the yield small, and the taxes generally unpopular. The re-enactment of an income tax law by South Carolina in 1897 meant simply a repetition of the old story. In 1908 a sixth state, Oklahoma, inaugurated a tax along the old lines from which the yield proved to be less than $5,000 a year. Meanwhile the Louisiana tax had disappeared.

An almost unanswerable argument against an unwieldy and unpopular revenue measure is produced when it can be shown that it yields to the state treasury only a few thousands of dollars annually,—hardly more than the cost of its collection if administrative machinery of any importance is required. Such an amount becomes almost microscopic when it is placed on the ten- and hundred-million dollar scale to which state business has grown during the last few years. Students of taxation became extremely sceptical of the success of state income taxes under any form of administration yet devised. The justice of the taxation of incomes was rarely questioned, but the practical difficulties of framing and administering a tax law which would apply equitably to income from various sources appeared insurmountable.

3. *Recent income tax legislation*

At the beginning of 1911 income tax laws were in force in only five states,—Massachusetts, North Carolina, South Carolina, Virginia, and Oklahoma. The Massachusetts tax was irregularly and unevenly enforced and was of no importance in the fiscal system of the state. In South Carolina and even in North Carolina the officials and the taxpayers resented the difficulties of collecting the taxes under the existing system and pointed to the small revenue as proof of the inadequacy of the tax. The Oklahoma measure was regarded as a failure by the state officials. In Virginia alone the income tax, which had risen to a yield of $130,000 by 1911, was regarded as a productive and valuable part of the state revenue system. The complete abandonment of this form of taxation by the states appeared to be only a matter of time.

Meanwhile an opposing tendency, for a long time unrecognized, was making itself felt in the continued efforts to reform the general property tax which were being made throughout the United States. The personal property tax in particular, because of its inadequacy and its increasingly unjust and pernicious results, was receiving more and more criticism. The states found themselves ready to experiment with classified property taxes, with inheritance, and even with income taxes, as possible avenues of relief from the unsatisfactory state of affairs in which the fiscal system of nearly every state was found.

As a result of the general and persistent attempts to improve state revenue systems the movement for the taxation of incomes spread until at the close of 1920 11 states had laws taxing personal incomes. The first indication of the changing point of view regarding state income taxes was given by the passage of an income tax law in Wisconsin in 1911. According to the terms of this law a heavy graduated tax was imposed upon the incomes of individuals and corporations from sources within the state. In 1912 Mississippi followed with a law modelled after the older type of state income-tax legislation. In 1915 Oklahoma made a fundamental revision of the law taxing incomes, following out some of the ideas which had proved workable in Wisconsin. Massachusetts passed an entirely new income tax law, of wide scope, in 1916, thereby abolishing the old income tax system which had survived from the period of colonial " faculty " taxes. Two experiments on a smaller scale were made in 1917 when Missouri and Delaware enacted personal income tax laws. Virginia revised the state income tax law in 1918, but without making important changes. The same year saw the only repeal of an income tax law of any permanence which occurred during the decade: South Carolina abolished the state income tax system and attempted to find no substitute for it. The year 1919 was one of unusual activity in the field of income taxes. New York, North Dakota, New Mexico, and Alabama passed laws taxing personal incomes, and North Carolina made important revisions in the existing law. The New York income tax, on account of the size of the incomes reached, appeared likely to prove the most significant in the history of income tax legislation. The New Mexico law was saved from repeal in 1920 only by the governor's veto. The Alabama law was declared unconstitutional early in 1920. . At the close of 1920 the list of states taxing personal incomes [1] stood as follows: Delaware, Massachusetts, Mississippi, Missouri, New Mexico, New York, North Carolina, North Dakota, Oklahoma. Virginia, and Wisconsin.

4. *The changed attitude towards the tax*

In the ten years which have passed since the income tax was adopted in Wisconsin the attitude of the best-known authorities has changed from scepticism to a tentative approval. Before 1911 the question of interest to students of taxation was not so much one of the possible success of state income taxes, for their elimination seemed only a question of time, but the underlying reasons for the consistency of the failures. In the light of our present knowledge it appears that the methods of administration of the tax, while seized upon by the more critical observers, were not sufficiently analyzed. In the first detailed study of state income taxes, made by Mr. Kinsman and published in 1903, the failure was laid at the door of administration, on four counts: [2]

The experience of the states with the income tax warrants the conclusion that the tax, as employed by them, has been unques-

---

[1] The plan of taxing the net income of corporations without correspondingly taxing the incomes of individuals had meanwhile been adopted by Connecticut (*Laws of 1915*, ch. 292), Montana (*Laws of 1917*, ch. 79), and West Virginia (*Laws of 1915*, ch. 3). In Connecticut the original tax was two per cent, in Montana one per cent, and in West Virginia one-half of one per cent. Before 1919 New York, with a three per cent tax on the net incomes of manufacturing and mercantile corporations, was included in this group. These states took advantage of the use of federal forms and the dates and machinery of the collection of the federal taxes, and found that the extremely low cost of collection was a distinct advantage of corporation taxes collected in this way. A number of other states taxed the incomes of certain specified classes of corporations.

[2] Kinsman, *op. cit.*, pp. 116, 117, 120, 121.

tionably a failure. It has satisfied neither the demands for justice nor the need of revenue. The question arises: Is this failure due to qualities inherent in the nature of the tax, or is it the result of conditions which may be removed? One of the fundamental principles of taxation is that the subjects of a state ought to contribute to the support of the government in proportion to their respective abilities, and it is generally agreed that these abilities are best measured by income. Therefore, theoretically at least, an income tax is unquestionably the fairest system yet proposed. . . .

While much of the legislation in the states relative to the income tax has been very unsatisfactory, often not appealing to the taxpayers' sense of justice and furnishing excuses for the concealment of property, nevertheless laws have been passed repeatedly which, if properly administered, would have distributed the burden with unusual justice. But these laws have failed quite as completely as those with provisions less satisfactory. The failure of the tax, therefore, can not have been due to the ill success of the laws in embodying the principle. . . .

As the result of our study we conclude that the state income tax has been a failure, due to the failure of administration, which, in turn, may be attributed to four causes—the method of self-assessment, the indifference of state officials, the persistent effort of the taxpayers to evade the tax, and the nature of the income. The tax can not be successful so long as taxpayers desirous of evading taxation are given the right of self-assessment. Since all attempts to change the method of self-assessment have failed and the nature of industry in the states is at present such as to make impossible the assessment of a general income tax at the source, we are forced to the conclusion that, even though no constitutional questions should arise, failure will continue to accompany the tax until our industrial system takes on such form as to make possible the use of some method other than self-assessment.

Writing six years later Mr. Kinsman noted a positive movement in the direction of the state taxation of personal incomes which escaped several of the students of that period. The movement was to have far-reaching effects in the next decade, but up to 1909 it had not shown itself in the passage of income tax legislation. The several reports of state tax commissions and other interested agencies and individuals *against* the tax were signs of interest in the device which were not to be disregarded. Moreover, the amendment to the Wisconsin constitution permitting the passage of an income tax law had already been adopted. Mr. Kinsman restated his position as follows:[1]

A study of the present period of income tax activity . . . affords the author no occasion to modify conclusions previously expressed. The current movement is not due to the success of the tax in any state, but rather to the spirit of reform now sweeping the country. This movement would hardly leave untouched the subject of taxation, where injustice is so common. The people have turned to an income tax because they believe in the theory that individuals should contribute to the support of the government according to ability, and that income is the most just measure of that ability. They expect success because they are possessed of the characteristic American optimism, and know little of the difficulties of administering such a law.

Mr. K. K. Kennan,[2] writing in Wisconsin in 1910, quoted with evident approbation passages from Mr. Kinsman's description of the difficulties of administering state income taxes, and added the following comment:[3]

It is a common remark that income tax laws are all right, but that they do not work in practice. Certainly the experiences of those states which have passed such laws are not encouraging, but is it not possible that the fault lies with the crude and imperfect administrative methods which have thus far been employed?

In the comprehensive volume on the income tax first

[1] D. O. Kinsman, "The Present Period of Income Tax Activity in the American States," *Quarterly Journal of Economics*, vol. xxiii (Feb., 1909), pp. 296-306.

[2] Mr. Kennan was later given the task of organizing and supervising the work of the income tax districts in Wisconsin.

[3] K. K. Kennan, *Income Taxation* (Milwaukee, 1910), pp. 235, 236, 323.

published in 1911 Professor E. R. A. Seligman characterized Mr. Kinsman's statements concerning the defects of
the administration of the state income tax laws as " unquestionably true " and enumerated other difficulties, such as
that of the localization of income, which must always be
met in working out a state income tax law.[1] Together with
several other tax experts, Professor Seligman was engaged at this time in working out the terms of a possible
federal income tax law, and he was undoubtedly influenced
both by the realization of the impracticability of efforts to
install successful state systems at a time when the federal
system was still undetermined and by a conviction of the
prime importance of a workable federal system.   In 1914
Professor Seligman commented on the success of the " improved and centralized administrative methods " which had
been so sucessfully used in the assessment and collection
of the income tax in Wisconsin, but continued to express
doubts as to the workability of income tax laws for all the
states.[2] By 1915, when the federal tax was in operation
and its successful working guaranteed, he was a supporter
of the project of a state income tax for New York.

During the same period various criticisms and a general
dissatisfaction with state income taxes had been expressed
in various official reports.   One of the most widely read
of these was the Report of the Massachusetts Commission
on Taxation of 1897, in which the existing law of Massachusetts was shown to be wholly unsatisfactory in its operation,[3] and the whole question of the administration of state
income taxes was described as an exceedingly difficult one.

---

[1] Seligman, *op. cit.*, pp. 426-429.

[2] Seligman, *op. cit.*, p. 429.

[3] Massachusetts Commission Appointed to Inquire into the Expediency
of Revising and Amending the Laws of the Commonwealth Relating to
Taxation, *Report*, 1897.

In New York in 1907 the report of the Special Tax Commission expressed criticism of the tax on four counts:[1]
first, the tax had always been a dismal failure; second, it
involved interstate complications; third, it would work
spasmodically and produce injustice and inquality; and,
fourth, it would lead to corruption. A third widely read
report in which state income taxes were severely criticised
was that of the California tax commission of 1906.[2]

A survey of the objections raised against the taxation of
personal incomes by the states, as these objections were
formulated before the change of sentiment manifested itself
in 1911, shows that the opposition was based largely on
the ground that all of the available evidence showed that
such taxes were extremely difficult to administer. The
theoretical virtues of the personal income tax as a means
of compelling the individual to contribute to the support of
the state government under which he lives in accordance
with his ability to pay were generally accepted as almost
ideal. The factors which had turned and kept public sentiment against the income tax were the petty yield, the
inequalities in administration, the character of the local
officials who had attempted to collect the taxes, and the low
repute in which personal income taxes had come to be held
in the states in which the experiment had been made.

The changing opinion as to the practicability of a levy on
incomes by the states became evident before any state of
importance fiscally speaking, with the exception of Wisconsin, had taken steps in the direction of new income
taxes. Professor Seligman's description of the new situation, given in connection with his early advocacy of a state
income tax for New York, was expressed as follows in his

[1] New York Special Tax Commission, *Report*, 1907, p. 46, *et seq.*

[2] Commission on Revenue and Taxation of the State of California,
Report, 1906.

presidential address at the Ninth Annual Conference of the
National Tax Association in 1915.[1]

Two events . . . have recently occurred to cause a reappraise-
ment of the situation. In the first place, great progress has been
made in the direction of a centralized state administration. In
New York we now have under the law of 1915 at all events a
distinct step in the direction of more efficient fiscal administration.
Of greater significance is the fact that the situation has been entirely altered by the introduction of the federal income tax. We
have now gotten people, and especially business people, accustomed to an income tax; and while there are still grave problems
to be solved and improvements to be secured, it may, I think, be
stated, without fear of contradiction, that the income tax has
come to stay and that in principle it is not seriously opposed by
the community. With the existence of this new tax, which is
successful so far as it goes, there arises the hitherto entirely un-
suspected prospect of a state income tax being able to lean up
against the federal tax, so as to avail itself of the federal returns
and to be able in this way to minimize a great part of the difficulties which would otherwise attach to an independent state income tax.

A year later Professor Bullock, whose efforts to bring
about the passage of the income tax law in Massachusetts
had reached a successful conclusion, expressed an opinion
that state income taxes were to be increasingly used, but
added a warning against too great a dependence upon
them: [2]

If every citizen were taxable at his domicile upon his entire income without exception or deduction, except such as may be
proper in the case of small incomes, and if then all tangible
property were taxed, under a proper classification, at its situs, we
should have the simplest, most logical, and most satisfactory of
all solutions. Everybody would pay an income tax in the locality
where he lives and enjoys the benefits of government, and all

[1] *Proceedings of the National Tax Association*, 1915, pp. 135, 136.
[2] *Proceedings of the National Tax Association*, 1916, pp. 383, 384.

property would contribute to the support of the jurisdiction where it receives the benefit of governmental services. . . .

But I am not greatly interested today in ultimate solutions. For good or ill, various states seem inclined to experiment with taxes on incomes, and it is important to understand the nature and the good or bad points of the income tax. It should not be regarded as a panacea, it is not going to replace all taxation of property, it must be carefully adjusted to existing taxes on tangible property and corporations, and it will certainly work badly if the rate is excessive or the administration decentralized. Finally, the state income tax should not be regarded as the rival, but rather as the complement or helpmate, of the classified property tax.

As the experience of the states with personal income taxes progressed, as administrative machinery was developed, and as lessons were learned and devices adapted from the federal government's use of the income tax, the workability of the state income taxes ceased to be a doubtful matter if administrative conditions were favorable. Many influences entered into the situation which are difficult of analysis. The effect upon the taxpayer's point of view of the continually increasing demands of the federal income tax as applied to individual incomes was undoubtedly a factor. This effect, although difficult to estimate, has probably been very great. The paths of the state officials responsible for the collection of state income taxes have almost certainly been smoothed by the annually recurring necessity of filling out the federal forms. The tendency towards evasion of the state taxes has probably been materially diminished by the publicity,—informal and unrecognized, but nevertheless existent—which has accompanied the payment of the federal tax, especially in the smalle, cities and towns. The effects of increasing prosperity upon the willingness of the individual to pay an income tax are also exceedingly difficult of measurement, but the " good times " were certainly not without effect.

The helpful influence of the federal tax system and the improvements in the form and administrative methods employed by the states made possible in turn further advances towards workable tax systems. It soon became apparent, as Professor Bullock saw clearly, that other improvements must parallel those of state income taxes if satisfactory revenue systems were to result. Increasing emphasis was laid upon the classification of property taxes and upon the usefulness of business or corporation taxes levied in a form like that of state income taxes but with a uniform rate. Within three years (1915 to 1917) New York, Connecticut, West Virginia, and Montana had adopted the latter plan. Professor Seligman, who with Professor Bullock was influential in framing the personal income tax law passed in New York in 1919, described the advantages of such a combination of income and business taxes in the annual address before the state tax conference held at Albany, in January, 1919:[1]

The advantages of this new system may be characterized as follows. The personal income tax coupled with an extension of the business tax is a far better measure of ability to pay taxes. . . . Second, the income tax is in conformity with modern economic conditions and is in this respect far preferable to the general property tax. Thirdly, the income tax reaches wealth that it would be impossible to reach by the property tax. . . . Fourthly, the income tax will bring about a more equitable adjustment as between classes and the State itself. An increase of the property tax which, as we know, necessarily implies a real estate tax, means an increase in the tax of the farmer; the adoption of the income tax will mean, as it ought to mean, primarily the taxation of the cities, where, as we have seen, most of the incomes are earned and received. . . .

It is clear, therefore, that from every point of view, that of ade-

[1] Eighth (New York) State Conference on Taxation, *Proceedings*, 1919, pp. 21, 22.

quacy, that of efficiency, and that of equity, all indications point unerringly to the desirability of the combination of an income tax and a business tax as a way out of our fiscal difficulties, both State and local.

5. *The development of model income tax laws*

The growing popularity of state income tax laws and the inevitability of interstate complications and confusion on account of those laws was one of the influences behind the appointment of a committee by the National Tax Association in 1916 to consider the report upon a model tax system. This committee was carefully chosen, and consisted of men whose interest in improved legislation and administration was already demonstrated.   Professor Bullock of Harvard was made chairman.   The entrance of the United States into the world war seriously interfered with the work of the committee during the first two years of its life: Professor T. S. Adams of Yale, one of the members, entered the employ of the United States Treasury Departmtnt as a revenue expert; Mr. Ogden Mills of New York City was sent at once to France; and the other members undertook such heavy additional duties during the war that the work of the committee was forced almost to a standstill.   Finally, in September, 1918, a preliminary report was published,[1] ('Appendix I), with the signatures of all members of the committee except Professor Adams, whose work at Washington had excluded him from collaboration in the report, but who described it as " one of the wisest and most helpful statements ever published concerning the proper structure of the tax system in an American state." [2]   The re-

---

[1] *Preliminary Report of the Committee Appointed by the National Tax Association to Prepare a Plan of a Model System of State and Local Taxation,* Sept., 1918.

[2] *Preliminary Report,* p. 45.

port met with " almost absolute approval " from the dele-
gates present at the annual conference of the National Tax
Association in June, 1919, and it may therefore confidently
be said that the endorsement of the principle of state income taxes which it contains is subscribed to by many of
the best-known tax administrators and tax critics in the
United States,

The committee reached the conclusion that a diversified
system of taxation was the only one which could be adapted
to present conditions. It was recognized that the proposed
system must yield large revenues, be practicable from an
administrative standpoint, be adapted to a federal form of
government, respect existing constitutional limitations, represent as nearly as possible a consensus of opinion, and
exclude measures wholly foreign to American ideas and
experience. The committee proposed three types of taxes :
a *personal income tax*, levied consistently upon the principle
of taxing every one at his place of domicile; a *property
tax upon tangible property*, levied objectively where such
property has its situs; and a *business tax* upon all business
carried on within the jurisdiction of the authority levying
such tax. The committee believed that in using a combination of these three taxes the states would be applying
logically and consistently the principles which already un-
derlay the greater part of their tax laws.

The recommendation of a personal income tax by this
committee, as a part of the three-fold tax system suggested
above, was the result of a choice among four possible forms
of personal taxation. The committee rejected the poll tax
as inadequate and unequal in its operation; a net property
tax, as foreign to the revenue traditions of the United
States; and a presumptive income tax, such as a tax on
rentals, as an imperfect indication of the individual's ability
to contribute to the support of the government under which

he lives. The committee considered that the fourth possible tax, the personal income tax, could be well administered, (as the experience of Wisconsin and Massachusetts had already proved at the time when the preliminary report was made) and offered the line of least resistance. The committee's conclusion on this point was tersely stated as follows: [1]

The committee . . . is of the opinion that a personal income tax is the best method of enforcing the personal obligation of the citizen for the support of the government under which he lives, and recommends it as a constituent part of a model system of state and local taxation.

With the caution that the details of each tax should be adjusted in such a way as to enable it to effect the principle on which it is based, the committee suggested " the broad outlines " of the manner in which the personal income tax should be levied, as follows:

First, since the personal income tax is to enforce the obligation of every citizen to the government under which he is domiciled, *the tax must be levied only upon persons and in the states where they are domiciled.* It should not apply to business concerns. If the personal income tax is not limited in this way, it will not form the supplement to the other taxes advocated, but will perpetuate the old evil of double taxation.

Second, the personal income tax should be levied in respect of the citizen's entire income from all sources. The only necessary qualification is that which is necessitated by the constitutional limitations upon taxation of federal bonds and the salaries of federal officials by the states. The personal obligation of the citizen to contribute to the support of the government under which he lives should not be affected by the form his investments take.

[1] *Preliminary Report,* p. 12.

Third, The personal income tax should be levied upon net income defined substantially as an accountant would determine it. This implies the deduction of operating expenses and interest on indebtedness. The large amount of federal bonds exempt from local taxation introduces a complication. The interest deduction should therefore be limited to an amount proportional to the income which the taxpayer derives from taxable sources.

Fourth, the amount of income exempted from the personal income tax should not exceed $600 for a single person and $1,200 for husband and wife, with $200 in addition for each dependent up to a number not to exceed three. This would make the maximum possible exemption $1,800. This recommendation is made with the modifying admission that conditions differ in the various states, and for that reason it is limited to the statement of the maximum exemptions desirable and the observation that under a democratic form of government as few people as possible should be exempt from the necessity of making a direct personal contribution towards the support of the state.

Fifth, the rate of the income tax should not be differentiated according to the sources from which income is derived. The personal income tax is designed to be part of a system in which there is a tax upon tangible property. Under such a system there will be heavier taxation of the sources from which funded income is derived, and there will be little, if any ground for attempting to differentiate the rates of the personal income tax. Furthermore, such differentiation greatly complicates the administration of the tax.

Sixth, the rates of taxation should be progressive, with the lowest rate not less than one per cent and the highest rate probably not greater than six per cent. The classes of taxable income to which the various rates apply should probably include $1,000 each. In such a plan, the tax for a single person would start at one per cent on any amount of income from $600 to $1,600 and reach six per cent on all income in excess of $5,600. This recommendation is made only in a general way, to illustrate the underlying recommendation that the rates of the personal income tax should be moderate, and should be, as nearly as practicable, uniform throughout the United States.

Seventh, the administration of the personal income tax should be placed in the hands of state officials. This type of administration is regarded by the committee as an indispensable condition for the successful operation of any state income tax. Experience has proved that local administration of the tax cannot work well. The state tax commission or commissioner is the proper agent to adminster the tax.

Eighth, the personal income tax should be collected from taxpayers, on the basis of returns, without attempts to collect at the source. Experience has shown that this can be done satisfactorily. Collection at the source presents serious administrative difficulties, imposes undeserved burdens on third parties, and sometimes tends to shift the tax burden. Collection at the source is inconsistent with the purpose of bringing home to the taxpayer his personal obligation to the government under which he lives. *Information* at the source may, however, prove helpful.

Ninth, the proceeds of the tax should probably be divided between the state and local governments in most cases. The plan of distribution is immaterial in the general plan of taxation which the committee advises. Moreover, the same solution is probably not advisable in every state. If the revenue is divided, the suggestion is made that the state governments might retain a proportion corresponding to the proportion which state expenditures bear to the total of the state and local expenditures, and that the same principle should apply in determining the share received by each of the subordinate political units. The entire question of distribution must necessarily be largely affected by local conditions, and the committee found it impossible to make other than general suggestions.

The business tax recommended by the committee was simply a moderate tax at a proportional rate (such as two per cent) upon the net income derived from business done in a particular locality.

The committee held that the combination of taxes recommended would give better results than any one tax. Inequalities which arise under the three separate taxes would not be concentrated at the same point, and there would almost certainly be a somewhat compensatory effect. The taxation of intangible property as property will be eliminated.

With regard to the amendment of state constitutions necessary for the introduction of these systems of taxation, the committee stated that "no more, and probably no less amendment of state constitutions" would be required than in the case of any other plan adequate to the needs of the case.

After the publication of the preliminary report of the committee on model taxation attention centered largely on the committee's conclusions concerning the personal income tax. Little adverse criticism was heard, but the immediate incorporation of such recommendations into law progressed slowly. In the New York personal income tax law of 1919 may be seen the expression of similar ideas concerning equitable rates and proper administrative procedure. To a lesser extent the laws passed in the same year in North Dakota and New Mexico show that the recommendations of the committee on model taxation have

been effective. In September, 1920, at the annual conference of the National Tax Association at Salt Lake City,
it developed that actual drafts of " model " personal income
tax and business income tax laws would be useful to state
officials who desired to have such laws considered by the
legislatures of 1921. The committee consented to undertake the work, obtained the assistance as counsel of Mr.
Henry H. Bond, of the Boston bar, who was in charge
of the administration of the Massachusetts income tax for
the first two years of its existence, and of Mr. George E.
Holmes, of the New York bar, author of a treatise on
federal taxation, and published the drafts of the two laws
early in 1921. These drafts were prepared with great care,
and an attempt was made to word the text and to number
the various articles and sections so that the corresponding
laws might be adopted by any state and subsequently enlarged or modified with a minimum of change.

The draft of a personal income tax law (Appendix II)
contains few changes from the plan suggested in the committee's preliminary report, although the details are necessarily presented much more fully. The exemptions suggested in the draft of the law are higher, and conform to
those permitted under the federal income tax law. The
final draft includes no suggestions for the distribution of
the proceeds of the tax, other than the suggestion that the
localities should be notified of their share in time to take
the sum into account in determining the local tax for the
year, and the suggestion that a reasonable amount should be
withheld for refunds. In presenting the draft, the chairman of the committee called attention to the fact that in such
matters of administration it was impossible to bring the
necessary provisions for the various states into the form of
one suggested law. The draft of the model income tax
law is in other respects full, detailed, and based on the best

modern income tax practice. The opportunity for flexibility in administrative matters which it offers makes its adoption in substantially its present form a practical possibility for almost every state.

The wave of popularity upon which the income tax has ridden during the past decade may subside to some extent, as it has subsided in the case of certain other features with which the American states have attempted to improve their revenue systems. Professor Lutz, who has been active in working for the adoption of an income tax in Ohio, gives the following warning:[1]

A few years ago separation of the sources of revenue was our revenue panacea. Today there is some danger of placing too great reliance upon the income tax as the chief agent of our fiscal salvation. Such expectations are doomed, and this failure will react unfavorably against the income tax in its proper place. It is more true today than ever that no one system will prove a cure-all. We must diversify our revenue system, combine property and income taxation, and strive toward a genuine and effective coördination of the widely diverse and different sources of revenue.

If such recommendations as these are followed, and if the personal income tax is fitted into its proper place in a diversified revenue system in the states in which it is adopted, we may expect only temporary reactions, and in the long run a permanent and stable place for the income tax in the state revenue systems.

[1] H. L. Lutz, *Report on the Operation of State Income Taxes*, in the *Report of the (Ohio) Special Joint Taxation Committee*, 1919, p. 125.

CHAPTER II

THE WISCONSIN INCOME TAX

1. *History of the legislation*

THE new phase in the taxation of incomes which opened with the adoption of an income tax in Wisconsin in 1911 was one of the results of years of effort for the reform of taxation in that state. Wisconsin's progressive attitude towards tax matters had become evident when the state tax commission was created in 1899. From that time forward the state had the advantage of the experience and advice of an able administrative organization with specialized functions, as a consequence of which several far-reaching improvements were brought about.

Agitation for an income tax had preceded the appointment of the commission by several years.[1] A progressive income tax plan had appeared in the platform of the People's Party in the early nineties, but no legislation had resulted.[2] The movement which culminated in the passage of an income tax law in 1911 first manifested itself in 1903, as a result of a discussion of the taxation of intangibles. In that year two members of the state tax commission re-

[1] The writer is indebted to Mr. Nils P. Haugen, who became a member of the Wisconsin Tax Commission in 1901 and who was its chairman from 1911 to 1921, for valuable information on the history of the income tax movement in Wisconsin.

[2] T. S. Adams, "The Wisconsin Income Tax," *American Economic Review*, vol. i, no. 4 (Dec., 1911), p. 906.

commended the exemption of credits from taxation. The
third member of the commission, Mr. Nils P. Haugen, opposed the flat exemption of credits without some substitute.
In the discussion of possible alternatives Mr. Haugen suggested an income tax. At that time the Wisconsin constitution did not provide directly for an income tax and it was
doubtful whether such a measure would be upheld; but the
suggestion had been brought into the public attention as a
live issue, and Mr. Haugen was requested by the assembly
committee on the assessment and collection of taxes to draft
a constitutional amendment permitting the imposition of a
graduated income tax. With the assistance of Mr. Dahl,
chairman of the committee on taxation, a draft was immediately made, and the legislature passed the amendment
in the same year (1903). Through an error in advertising
the amendment the next step was postponed for two years.
The amendment was again approved by the legislatures of
1905 and 1907. It was voted upon by the people in the
elections of November, 1908, and carried by an overwhelming majority. Two bills were introduced in the legislature
of 1909,—one in the senate by Senator Paul Husting, later
United States Senator, and the other in the assembly by
Mr. Ingram. Both bills represented Mr. Haugen's income
tax recommendations. Meanwhile a campaign of popular
education had been proceeding; the subject was given wide
publicity, and Mr. Haugen himself was a frequent contri-
butor to the *Milwaukee Free Press,* writing in support of
the proposed tax.

After a discussion of the two bills proposed in the legislature of 1909, the bills were referred to a special legislative
committee which was instructed to report to the legislature
of 1911. The committee presented a bill to the legislature
of 1911, and after another prolonged discussion and the introduction of several amendments the bill became law in the

summer of 1911,[1]—eight years after the proposal was first made by Mr. Haugen.

In drafting the income tax law all of the available information concerning state income taxes and the income taxes of foreign countries was reviewed in great detail, and the Wisconsin law was painstakingly framed along the lines which history had shown to be most workable.   Two Wisconsin men, Professor D. O. Kinsman and Mr. K. K. Kennan, had published historical studies of income taxes which were extensively used in the preparation of the Wisconsin bills.[2]   Professor Kinsman regarded state income taxes as almost complete failures, but his account of low rates and local administration as possible causes of the failure was illuminating.   The Prussian income tax was in operation at this time, and Norway was working on a proposal which was subsequently enacted into law.   Although few of the particular provisions which were found in these measures were applicable to the situation in Wisconsin, the careful analysis of the various explanations of successes and failures which was made by the proponents of the Wisconsin tax must be held in part responsible for the seaworthiness of the Wisconsin law which was finally passed in 1911.

Professor T. S. Adams, one of the early supporters of the income tax in Wisconsin, notes as significant the fact that the ratification of the constitutional amendment was urged by all political parties and that in 1910 the passage of an income tax law called for in the various party platforms.[3]   Professor Adams holds that this agreement on the income tax represented the fusion of two groups: those

[1] *Laws of Wisconsin*, 1911, ch. 658 (June 29, 1911).

[2] D. O. Kinsman, *The Income Tax in the Commonwealths of the United States* (New York, 1903) ; and K. K. Kennan, *Income Taxation* (Milwaukee, 1910).

[3] Adams, *op. cit.*, pp. 906, 907.

who believed income taxation to be a means of social reform, and those who regarded the tax merely as a practical substitute for personal property taxation.

By the time the income tax law was finally passed the situation with regard to the taxation of personal property had become serious. Governor McGovern, during whose administration the tax was put into operation, and to whom is due much of the credit for the success of the income tax in its critical first year, describes the old system of personal property taxation as follows:[1]

The reason an income tax was demanded by the people of Wisconsin was that the old system of personal property taxation had broken down. . . . Irregularities in the assessment of property inevitably destroyed uniformity of taxation, but they did more. They introduced a vicious system of class legislation. A careful investigation of the assessments of 2,239 persons shows that if the assessment of the property of farmers be placed at 100 per cent, that of merchants would be only 64 per cent and that of manufacturers but 36 per cent. . . . Worse still, the poor were systematically discriminated against in favor of the rich. The plain fact is that under this system the poorer a man was the higher proportionately he was assessed, and the richer he was the lower he was assessed.

The income tax law passed in 1911 was unlike many of the state income tax laws which had been tried in this country in that it provided for the taxation of business as well as of personal incomes. The incomes of corporations and of individuals (resident and non-resident) arising from sources within the state of Wisconsin were subject to taxation. The law provided that the term " income " should include rent, interest, wages, profits, royalties, and " all other gains, profits or income of any kind derived from any source whatever " (except those specifically exempted).

[1] F. E. McGovern, "A State Income Tax," *Proceedings of the Governors' Conference*, 1912, pp. 80, 82.

Residents of the state were entitled to exemptions of $800 to the individual, $1,200 to husband and wife together, and $200 for each child and for each other dependent. Various kinds of income not properly subject to taxation in this way, such as pensions from the United States and dividends from corporations which paid the income tax, were also exempted. Deductions were allowed for the ordinary expenses of doing business and for similar items. The law included a provision that in the payment of income taxes it should be allowable to present personal property tax receipts. This provision, known as the " personal property tax offset " was to become a serious problem in later years.

Progressive rates were applied to both individual and corporate incomes. The tax on individual incomes, which reached a maximum at six per cent on amounts in excess of $12,000, was less steeply graduated. The following table, adapted from that published by the State Tax Commission as an aid to computation, shows the scheduled rates and true rates of the tax.[1]

Taxable Income of Individuals	Rate (per cent)	Tax	Total tax	True rate (per cent) on whole amount
1st $1,000.........	1	$10.00	$10.00	1.0
2nd 1,000.........	1¼	12.50	22.50	1.125
3rd 1,000.........	1½	15.00	37.50	1.25
4th 1,000.........	1¾	17.50	55.00	1.375
5th 1,000.........	2	20.00	75.00	1.5
6th 1,000.........	2½	25.00	100.00	1.6667
7th 1,000.........	3	30.00	130.00	1.8571
8th 1,000.........	3½	35.00	165.00	2.0625
9th 1,000.........	4	40.00	205.00	2.2778
10th 1,000.........	4½	45.00	250.00	2.5
11th 1,000.........	5	50.00	300.00	2.7273
12th 1,000.........	5½	55.00	355.00	2.9582
13th 1,000.........	6	60.00	415.00	3.1923
15th 1,000.........	6	60.00	535.00	3.5667
20th 1,000.........	6	60.00	835.00	4.175

[1] Wisconsin Tax Commission, *The Wisconsin Income Tax Law* (1919), p. 26.

The rates for the income of corporations, as originally adopted, were determined by the relation between the taxable income and the assessed value of the property used in the acquisition of the income. The scale was graduated, rising from one half of one per cent where the per cent of taxable income to value of property was one per cent or less, to six per cent where the per cent of taxable income to value of property was from 11 to 12 per cent.

This method proved to be unnecessarily unwieldy, and after two years the scheme was changed to correspond with that used for the calculation of taxes on individual incomes.[1] The initial rate was fixed at two per cent, and the maximum of six per cent was reached at a point just above $6,000.

Probably the most distinctive feature of the Wisconsin law was the centralized administration for which it provided. The state tax commission was required to assess the incomes of corporations and to provide the necessary rules for the assessment of the incomes of individuals and partnerships; to divide the state into assessment districts, and to appoint officials under the civil service rules to make the assessments within the respective districts. A state "supervisor of the income tax" was appointed to work out the details of the new system.

The collections were made through the local collectors of property taxes. The income taxes were certified to these collectors, and were entered for collection at the same time and in the same manner as other taxes, but on a separate roll. In this way the persons who might find the remission of the amount of their taxes to the state treasurer an unfamiliar and difficult process were enabled to pay the required amounts to the local collector through a simple transfer of cash.

[1] *Laws of Wisconsin*, 1913, ch. 720.

Several new problems of taxation were produced by the Wisconsin law. One of the most puzzling was that of the allocation of income derived from within and without the state. Income from rentals, royalties, and gains or profits from the operation of any farm, mine, or quarry was not apportionable for the reason that it followed the *situs* of the property from which it was derived. Income from personal services, land contracts, mortgages, stocks, bonds, and securities was not apportionable for the reason that it was considered to have its *situs* at the residence of the recipient. Business incomes of individuals derived from sources within and without the state were subject to tax only upon that portion received from sources within the state. In determining this amount the rule of apportionment for individuals followed that for corporations, which stood as follows after 1913:[1]

In determining the proportion of capital stock employed in the state, the same shall be computed by taking the gross business in dollars of the corporation in the state and add[ing] the same to the full value in dollars of the property of the corporation located in the state. The sum so obtained shall be the numerator of a fraction of which the denominator shall consist of the total gross business in dollars of the corporation, both within and without the state, added to the full value in dollars of the entire property of the corporation, both within and without the state. The fraction so obtained shall represent the proportion of capital stock represented within the state.

Having obtained this figure (for example, .6), the corresponding part of the net income was taxable in Wisconsin.

A system of "information at the source" was developed into a smoothly working part of the machinery early in the history of the Wisconsin income tax. This system is

[1] *Laws of Wisconsin*, 1913, ch. 720 [section 1770b, subsection 7, subdivision (e)].

only partially provided for in the income tax law itself, but it has been worked out by the tax commission under the authority which it holds for making necessary regulations. The law provides that in order to deduct wages paid to employees from gross income, corporations must report " the name, address and amount paid each such employee or officer residing within this state to whom a compensation of seven hundred dollars or more shall have been paid during the assessment year." [1]   In the same way the names and addresses of persons to whom interest on indebtedness is paid must be reported or the deduction of such interest will not be permitted to the taxpayer.[2]   As the plans have been worked out, the forms distributed for the income tax returns are accompanied by blanks upon which salaries or wages to the amount of $700 or more are to be entered, and by other blanks for lists of stockholders of corporations and the dividends paid them.   In the same way reports are made concerning interest payments.   This system operates as a check upon the payment of excessive salaries by corporations, as a means of checking up corporate deductions for wages, salaries, and dividends, and as a check upon the returns made by individuals who receive wages, salaries, dividends, or interest.   This method was at first regarded as highly inquisitorial, but with the passage of time the return of such information has come to be regarded as a matter of course and as one of the troublesome but necessary details in the efficient administration of an income tax.

The distribution of the proceeds of the income tax has proved to be one of the most vexing problems which the levy of income taxes by the states has produced.   Up to the time of the passage of the Wisconsin law the matter had had little discussion, and the funds had gone into the various

[1] *Laws of Wisconsin*, 1913, ch. 720.
[2] *Laws of Wisconsin*, 1917, ch. 231.

state treasuries as a matter of course. Wisconsin, however, adopted a novel plan of distribution to the localities. It was hoped that the income tax would eventually supplant the more undesirable forms of personalty taxation, and in that case some recompense must be made to the local taxing units. The Wisconsin law accordingly provided that 70 per cent of the receipts from the income tax should go to the city, town, or village from which those receipts were derived; 20 per cent to the county, and the remaining 10 per cent to the state. It was assumed that the sum retained by the state would approximately cover the cost of collection. In practice, the state's share of the receipts have far exceeded the cost.

The two assumptions underlying this plan,—that of a large revenue from the tax and the belief that the tax would prove an effective substitute for the personal property tax—were subsequently justified. The distribution to the localities proved to be a workable arrangement and one which other and richer states were later to experiment with.

Further evidence that the Wisconsin income tax was intended as a substitute for the tax on personal property rather than as an addition to the general property tax is found in the fact that the original bill provided for the entire exemption of personal property. The legislators feared that the proceeds of the income tax would not compensate for the losses which would result, and it was decided that the taxation of tangible personal property should be continued, but that the taxes paid should be allowed as " offsets " against the income tax, in the manner described above. Intangibles were exempted, however, together with certain classes of property which had proved to be particularly difficult of assessment, such as household goods and furnishings, farm machinery, implements and tools, and certain other minor classes of tangible personal property.

The gloomy predictions of the early failure of the Wisconsin income tax came to nothing. The constitutionality of the law was soon attacked, but it was upheld.[1] In 1913 it became necessary to make the change in the method of taxing the income of corporations which has been described, but otherwise the law remained unchanged in its essentials until 1919. The so-called " inquisitorial " character of income tax legislation, which was made the basis of one of the arguments used against the tax, as a matter of fact was rarely resented. Little evidence has been found of attempts to defraud.[2]

From 1919 to the present a tendency to experiment with the income tax system has shown itself in Wisconsin. In 1919 the question of raising soldiers' bonuses was under consideration. The income tax, productive in the past, particularly in the later war years, seemed to offer a fruitful field, and it was agreed that the existing system could be utilized for raising a large sum of money in a very short time. During the regular session of the legislature a soldiers' bonus act was passed, containing the provision that the necessary funds were to be collected in part from income and in part from property.[3] In the case of the tax on individual incomes, the *soldiers' bonus surtax,* as it was called, was obtained by doubling the rates in each $1,000 of income with the exception of the first $3,000 of taxable income. At the same time the corporation income tax rates were doubled. This proposal came at a time when the high federal income tax rates were under a heavy fire of criticism, but the trend of popular opinion was such that a referendum brought an overwhelming majority for the tax.

[1] *Income Tax Cases*, 148 Wis. 456.

[2] K. K. Kennan, " The Wisconsin Income Tax," *Annals of the American Academy*, vol. lviii (March, 1915), pp. 75, 76.

[3] *Laws of Wisconsin*, 1919, ch. 667.

Later in 1919 a second increase was made. In a special session of the legislature an educational bonus act was passed, appropriating an amount equal to one-fifth of the original bonus to men and nurses who who served in the late war, to be used for purposes of education.[1] The second surtax was computed by adding one-fifth of the soldiers' bonus surtax to that tax in the case of both individuals and corporations. The tax was to be collected for five years.

In spite of the dangers of treating the income tax as a source of unlimited revenue to be drawn upon at will, particularly at a time when federal income taxes were under constant attack, proposals for increasing the Wisconsin income tax were put before the legislature of 1921. The place of the income tax in the state revenue system showed signs of becoming a political issue, with the conservative interests of the state aligned against the increases.

A change in the Wisconsin practice was made necessary when the United States Supreme Court rendered a decision, on March 1, 1920, to the effect that the provision of the New York income tax law which denied to nonresidents the exemptions permitted to residents was discriminatory and unconstitutional. Wisconsin had formerly permitted the individual exemptions only to residents, and although the Wisconsin Supreme Court had expressed grave doubts as to the constitutionality of the provision, action had been delayed until a concrete case should be brought. After the New York decision was rendered the tax commission considered that it was equally binding upon Wisconsin, and ruled that in computing taxable income non-residents should be allowed the same exemptions as those to which they would be entitled if they were residents of the state.

[1] Wisconsin Tax Commission, *The Wisconsin Income Tax Law* (1919), pp. 60-62.

2. *The financial history of the tax*

The Wisconsin income tax was a financial success from the first. When the law went into effect the opponents of the plan made gloomy predictions of the probable yield, and even the advocates of the tax could not guarantee that an untried revenue measure would prove its worth in the first year.[1]

It was freely prophesied that Wisconsin would only duplicate the experiences of other states and that the amount collected would scarcely suffice to pay the cost of collection. Even the friends of the measure did not estimate the probable yield at over one million dollars, and it was realized that the administration of the tax would be attended by many peculiar difficulties in the first year of its operation. Under those circumstances there was no small surprise when it was found that the income tax levy of the first year . . . amounted to the very respectable sum of $3,591,161.46.

The record of succeeding years shows that this amount was a minimum which has been several times multiplied as changes have occurred in the taxable income of the state and as the administration of the tax has been improved. The figures for the " income tax levy " used by Mr. Kennan in estimating the productiveness of the tax must be pared down when the actual cash yield to the state is desired, for the personal property tax offset has been so extensively used in paying income taxes that the original income tax levy has sometimes been cut in half. The record of cash paid in (excluding the personal property tax offsets) during the period covered by the operation of the law is as follows:[2]

[1] Kennan, *op. cit.*, p. 73.
[2] Wisconsin Tax Commission, *Report*, 1920, p. 32.

Year of assessment (on incomes of previous year)	Cash collections
1912	$1,631,413
1913	1,935,847
1914	2,002,213
1915	1,906,442
1916	2,998,767
1917	6,037,719
1918	6,951,483
1919	6,243,376

The conspicuous increases which first became apparent in the collections for the assessment year 1917 were regarded by the state tax commission as " abnormal " and " due to abnormal business conditions." The commission's warning that " the permanent value of income taxation " could not be " judged by the returns for these abnormal years " [1] furnishes one of the instances of the scepticism of the possibilities of income taxation which still exists even on the part of those who support the tax.

Estimates of the financial success of the income tax in Wisconsin require the separation of the revenue from the tax on the incomes of individuals from the proceeds of the tax on the income of corporations, as the taxation of individual incomes is now regarded to be a distinct question and one which is believed to demand separate legislation. Figures furnished by the Wisconsin tax commission show that the levy on the income of individuals has formed from one-third to one-fourth of the total levy throughout the greater part of the period of the operation of the tax.[2] In the assessment of 1920 the levy on personal incomes represented almost exactly one-third of the total levy, exclusive of the amounts assessed as soldiers' bonus surtaxes. In the assessment of 1919 the corresponding fraction was one-fourth.

[1] *Report*, 1918, p. 5.
[2] *Report*, 1920, p. 61.

The real significance of the revenue from the income tax in Wisconsin can be appreciated only by means of a comparison with other income taxes, particularly the federal income tax, and with the other sources of state revenue. On the assumption that the actual cash collections in Wisconsin are derived from individuals and corporations in approximately the same ratio as the original levies, individuals paid in cash as taxes to the state of Wisconsin about $1,600,000 on incomes received in 1918. The federal government's collections on individual incomes in Wisconsin for that year amounted to $11,382,000 or about seven times as much as the state collections.[1]

A satisfactory comparison of the revenue from the Wisconsin income tax and the other sources of state revenue cannot be made, since Wisconsin distributes the major part of the proceeds of the tax to the local units instead of retaining them as a part of the state funds. If the state absorbed all the income tax receipts in addition to its ordinary revenue, the ratio of income tax collections to total state receipts would be (roughly) one to five. Even with the 10 per cent share of the proceeds which the law assigns to the state itself the surplus for the state is large. This percentage, originally intended to cover merely the cost of administration, has yielded in the last three years more than $600,000 annually, while the cost of collection was estimated at approximately $160,000 in 1919-1920.[2]

The low cost of collecting the income tax has been emphasized by the Wisconsin officials from the time when the results of the tax first became apparent. Within the first two or three years it was discovered that the 10 per cent of the proceeds which was assigned to the state not only

---

[1] United States Internal Revenue, *Statistics of Income for 1918*, p. 24.
[2] Wisconsin Tax Commission, *Report*, 1920, p. 65.

covered the cost of collection but defrayed the entire expense of all of the activities of the state tax commission.[1] On the basis of cash collections the cost has ranged from one to nearly three per cent.[2] On the basis of assessments this figure for the cost of collection appears very much lower. The presentation of personal property tax receipts as offsets, a practice which does away with nearly one-half of the tax payments which would otherwise be made, is a process which requires accounting and is represented by an administrative cost but which reduces the cash amounts on the basis of which the administrative costs are estimated in percentages. As a result the cost appears larger than it would otherwise be. A further difficulty in estimating the cost exactly is the fact that the local treasurers collect the income tax with practically no increase in compensation.

A second method of judging the cost of collection is that of estimating the cost of each return handled. In 1920, 206,626 individual returns and 12,000 corporation returns were filed. The cost of administration of this division of the tax commission's work, reported as approximately $160,000 for the year, means a cost per return of about $.75.

Throughout its operation the income tax in Wisconsin has been primarily an urban tax. Milwaukee alone contributes almost one-half of the revenue from the tax. Farmers paid only 13.6 per cent of the tax on 1919 incomes.[3] Probably less than one-half of the rural population is liable to the tax, for the small cash profits from farming operations and the numerous exemptions combine to exclude a large part of the agricultural population from the act. On

[1] T. E. Lyons, " The Wisconsin Income Tax," *Annals of the American Academy*, vol. lviii (March, 1915), p. 82.

[2] Wisconsin Tax Commission, *Reports*, 1914, p. 126; 1916, p. 69; 1920, p. 65.

[3] *Report*, 1920, pp. 34, 64.

the other hand, city workers with moderate incomes do not escape. The largest single number of the individuals assessed (one-fourth of the whole number) were mechanics and tradesmen. These individuals paid more than one-fifth of the total amount of taxes on personal incomes for 1919.

A comparison of the Wisconsin tax with the federal tax shows that the proportion of the income taxes paid by the poorer people is somewhat greater in Wisconsin than in the country as a whole,[1] a fact which is the natural conse-quence of the lower exemptions under the Wisconsin law and of the fact that Wisconsin is the state of residence of relatively few of the largest individual income taxpayers in the country.

Another anomaly which has been observed in Wisconsin has a wholly different origin. The provision of the Wisconsin law that 70 per cent of the income taxes derived from property or business in a given locality shall be paid to the district has resulted in curious situations in certain rural districts where few individuals are liable to the income tax.[2] Heavy income taxes were paid in certain small rural districts of this kind as the result of the operations of manufacturing establishments located within their borders. The local communities contributed little to the income of such establishments, but in a few cases they received extravagantly large sums when the proceeds of the tax were distributed, particularly during the war boom. The appropriation of a larger part of the proceeds of the income tax by the state and the limitation of the amount payable to a locality to a certain percentage of the assessed valuation are two of the remedies which have been suggested.

---

[1] *Cf.* United States Internal Revenue, *Statistics of Income for 1918,* p. 21, and Wisconsin Tax Commission, *Report,* 1920, p. 33.

[2] T. E. Lyons, " Distribution of Income Taxes to Localities," *Bulletin of the National Tax Association,* vol. v, no. 3 (Dec., 1919), pp. 73-75.

3. *The outlook for the income tax in Wisconsin*

After nearly a decade of operation the success of the income tax in Wisconsin seems to be beyond question. The statement of the state tax commission in 1918, made without foreknowledge of the extensions which the tax was to undergo in 1919, shows an appreciation of the productive power of this form of taxation.[1]

Results have been satisfactory. . . . The increase in the tax is not confined to any particular locality or localities but is general throughout the state. The gradual and steady increase under normal conditions is doubtless due, first, to the fact that under such conditions there is a steady growth in business from year to year throughout the state and, second, because of the increased efficiency in administration. The conclusion from the foregoing is that a constant increase in revenue from income taxation may be confidently expected, subject of course to fluctuations due to occasional abnormal expansion or contraction of business.

The policy of utilizing the income tax to raise large sums of money for purposes other than the permanent needs of the state and the localities has already been questioned. Aside from the difficulties of assessing and collecting these taxes—difficulties which proved to be serious for the Wisconsin officials, owing largely to the haste in which the work was required to be done—the raising of such funds as temporary soldiers' bonuses through this means may tend to produce dissatisfaction with the tax. The separate reference to the Wisconsin tax as the " soldiers' bonus surtax " is a minor aspect of the matter which has undoubtedly made clear the purpose of the additions and prevented unthinking dissatisfaction on the part of the least informed of the taxpayers. Even with all possible care, however, it is dangerous to regard incomes as an unlimited source of revenue for all purposes.

[1] Wisconsin Tax Commission, *Report*, 1918, p. 5.

In order to reach the maximum efficiency the state tax
commission held that the Wisconsin income tax law as it
stood at the opening of the year 1921 must be amended in
several important particulars.   The most pressing necessity
was believed to be that of the repeal of the provision allowing the personal property tax offset in the payment of income taxes.   The tax commission urged the repeal of this
provision in its biennial reports of 1916, 1918, and 1920.
This provision, originally incorporated in the law " with
the idea of accomplishing without too violent a shock to taxing machinery the substantial elimination of personal property taxation and the substitution therefor of ability taxation " came to be considered an incongruous feature of the
tax system.   The ninth biennial report of the state tax
commission contained a description of the inequalities which
resulted from the retention of the provision: [1]

The absurdity of requiring taxpayers to make elaborate and
complicated reports of their income and of maintaining an expensive organization to assess it, only to have the result nullified
by the presentation of personal property tax receipts, is too plain
to require argument. If it is the settled policy of the state to tax
personal property, then no reason is apparent why the owner
thereof should be favored as compared with the owner of real
estate.   To do so is to perpetuate discrimination between the
owners of different classes of property.

Aside from this inequality the offset provision offers constant
inducement to false classification in making the assessment. It is
to the interest of those having income taxes to pay to have as
large a personal property offset as possible, and local assessors
are constantly urged to assess fixed machinery, permanent buildings on leased land and other forms of real estate as personalty
for the purpose of offset.

The urgent appeals of the commission were not without
effect, and at the time of the 1919 session of the legisla-

[1] Wisconsin Tax Commission, *Report*, 1918, p. 7.

ture the taxation committee of the assembly held hearings on the question of repealing the offset provision. The business interests of the state appeared to be almost united in opposing the repeal. The principal argument against the repeal was that it would greatly increase the taxes of the persons with large incomes.

The report of the state tax commission for the year 1920 contained a detailed summary of the arguments for the repeal of the offset provision, reinforced by statistical summaries of the effect of the use of the offset upon cash collections from the income tax.[1] This summary shows that in the course of the eight years of the collection of the income tax $23,000,000 or more than 43 per cent of the collections on income taxes was paid by the presentation of personal property tax receipts. The provision was made use of more extensively in the cities than in the towns and villages.

The offset provision was acknowledged to have been introduced to facilitate the elimination of the personal property tax through the income tax. It was assumed that upon the passage of the income tax law the taxation of personal property in Wisconsin would be practically eliminated. Experience through a period of years showed, on the contrary, that the income tax with the adjunct of the offset was in no way displacing the personal property tax. The assessment of personal property steadily increased after the income tax law was adopted

The objections urged by the state tax commission in 1920 was summarized as follows:

First, the offset provision is entirely foreign to any true conception of income taxation and tends to defeat rather than to promote that form of taxation.

Second, it is wholly inconsistent with " ability taxation."

[1] Wisconsin Tax Commission, *Report,* 1920, pp. 31-43.

Third, it deprives the state and the municipalities therein of large revenue to which they are justly entitled.

Fourth, it favors those best able to pay and is discriminating between taxpayers.

Fifth, in administration it entails a waste of public funds.

Further changes in the Wisconsin income tax law recommended to the legislature of 1921 were as follows:

The incorporation in the Wisconsin law of a provision taxing all the incomes of residents whether earned at home or abroad.

A change in the section providing for family exemptions so that the Wisconsin law might be brought into harmony with the decision of the Supreme Court of the United States [1] declaring the denial of exemptions to non-residents discriminatory and the provision therefore null and void.

The taxation of bank dividends under the income tax law.

An increase in the rate of tax on individual incomes to correspond at least with the rate in force on corporation incomes.

In addition, the question of including under the income tax law the considerable number of groups of corporations whose income was wholly exempt from taxation by express statute—namely banks, public service corporations of all kinds, and several other groups—was submitted to the legislature for consideration.

The occasion for the reconsideration of the exclusion of certain large classes of corporations from the income tax is to be found in the fact that the period of declining incomes has arrived, according to the state tax commission. Since the original income tax law was adopted the character of succeeding income tax legislation has been progressively limiting to the scope of the law. New deductions have

[1] Travis *vs.* Yale & Towne Manufacturing Co., 252 U. S. 60.

been granted, old deductions have been enlarged, and the term "income" has been restricted so as to exclude receipts which were previously taxable. The tax commission does not criticise the individual amendments in particular, but emphatically calls attention to the fact that " almost any amendment offered which would in any way lighten the burdens of income taxpayers has been enacted, while amendments suggested that would tend to increase the revenue from income taxation have been rejected." It is plain, the report continues, that " if this process of elimination of taxable incomes goes on long enough and no substitute is adopted, the Wisconsin income tax law will become a mere shadow." [1] With the decline in incomes after the return to peace conditions there is liable to be a falling-off in the net returns from the income tax unless this trend of legislation is recognized in all its aspects and steps are taken to counterbalance it. For this reason several of the recommendations made to the legislature of 1921 are concerned with methods of expanding the revenue from the income tax.

The movement to include under the tax all income of residents wherever derived is one which, if successful, will bring Wisconsin into line with the states which have recently adopted income taxes. Even Massachusetts and North Carolina, which tax income of specified kinds only, apply those taxes to the income of residents whatever the source from which such income is derived.

The commission's recommendation that the rate of taxation on individual incomes should be increased to correspond with that on corporation incomes has little to support it at the present juncture. The commission " can see no reason why an income whether received by a corporation and individual should not bear the same rate just as the same rate

[1] *Report*, 1920, p. 46.

of taxation is applied to real and personal property whether owned by an individual or corporation." [1] The inapplicability of a comparison between income and property for purposes of taxation according to ability is generally admitted, however, and needs one exposition here. The objections to the commission's plan are two: first, the rates on individual incomes are already unusually high in Wisconsin, and their increase at a time when the federal rates are still high is of extremely doubtful expediency; second, the justice and desirability of the imposition of identical rates for individual and corporate incomes are not matters which can be so easily settled. The committee on model taxation is of the opinion that the " business tax " (in effect largely a corporation income tax) should be regarded as a mode of taxation quite distinct from the taxation of personal incomes, and that different scales of rates are justifiable. The committee's suggestions for the proposed business tax in almost no way correspond to the present corporation income tax in Wisconsin, a fact which suggests that using this tax as a kind of norm might be fraught with difficulty in the future.

Although the Wisconsin income tax is undoubtedly in need of certain amendments along the lines of some of those which have been suggested by the state commission, in order to be brought into adjustment with present income tax practice in this country and with financial affairs within the state, the success and the historical significance of the law can hardly be overstimated. The leaders of the income tax movement took a bold step at a time when the state income tax was in disrepute in this country among the men who had tried to administer it and among the students of taxation who had analyzed its history as a revenue-producer. With the use of great skill and a willingness to learn from the

[1] *Report, 1920*, p. 45.

experience of other states anad other countries, the first
law was drafted in such a way that the principal pitfalls of
American state income taxes of the past were avoided: the
rates were made sufficiently high, the tax was made a
general income tax, and a new type of centralized administration, safeguarded from political exploitation as far as
possible, was devised. In view of the care with which the
system was planned, it is not strange that Wisconsin was
the first state to make the income tax a smoothly working
fiscal measure and at the same time a source of great revenue.

The excellence of many of the provisions of the original
Wisconsin law is now widely recognized. In the preparation of a draft of a model personal income tax law (Appendix II) the National Tax Association's committee on a
model system of state and local taxation utilized many por-
tions of the Wisconsin law, and followed fairly closely the
outline of administration which has been perfected in Wisconsin, for it is this field that Wisconsin's contribution
has been the greatest. The best modern opinion has now
turned against rates as high as those used in Wisconsin, is
opposed to limiting the incomes taxed to those derived
within the state, and is unconditionally against the use of
such devices as the personal property tax offset; but the
superiority of Wisconsin's administrative machinery has
never been questioned. It would hardly be an exaggera-
tion to say that the success of state income taxes in the last
few years of their history has been due largely to the
adaptation and use of the plan of centralized and specialized
administration of the state income tax which was first used
by Wisconsin in 1911.

CHAPTER III

The Taxation of Incomes in Mississippi and Oklahoma

The adoption of the income tax by Wisconsin in 1911 had far-reaching consequences for other states as well as for Wisconsin itself, but these influences required time in which to make themselves felt. The law which was the immediate successor of the Wisconsin income tax law, that of Mississippi, showed no traces of the experiment which was going on in the north. Mississippi, unlike many of the southern states, had had no experience with the early faculty taxes or with Civil War income taxes. Property taxes and privilege taxes made up the greater part of the revenue. The latter proved unsatisfactory and unequal, as they have so generally become where they are extensively used, and in 1912 it was decided that the income tax should be tried out. Unfortunately the tax was modelled after that of the nearest neighbor with an income tax, Oklahoma, which had been trying to collect a tax of the older type, and the Wisconsin devices were ignored. Apparently the law was handicapped from the beginning. In addition to the defects of the Oklahoma type of law to which Mississippi fell heir, the Mississippi law of 1912 contained an error in phrasing which could not be remedied until 1914,[1] so that its operation was delayed.

---

[1] *Laws of Mississippi*, 1912, ch. 101 ; 1914, ch. 116.

1. *The present Mississippi tax*

By the terms of the act of 1912, which is still in force, a tax of one-half of one per cent is levied upon all individual incomes in excess of $2,500. Expenses of doing business and *ad valorem* taxes paid may be deducted from income. The proceeds go to the general state fund. The enforcement of the law and the other duties of administration are left to the state auditor and the regular county assessors.

The Mississippi income tax has never yielded a large revenue. Before 1918 the tax could never be counted upon to yield more than $25,000.[1] In later years, with the growth of money incomes in the country, the receipts have more than doubled, but they still form only a very small percentage[2] of the total tax receipts of the state.

Year	Income tax receipts [3]
1918	$31,123
1919	51,426
1920	68,877

The small return from the income tax in Mississippi is brought out even more clearly by a comparison with the amounts collected in Mississippi by the federal government in a corresponding period. The federal income tax receipts from the state for 1918 were $3,542,849,[4] or more than 100 times as great as the state collections.

The cost of administering the income tax in Mississippi is not separately calculated, for the matter is handled by officials who are elected for other duties. That part of the

---

[1] *Joint Report of the (Mississippi) Senate and House Committee to Consider the State's Revenue System and Fiscal Affairs, Submitted to the Regular Session of 1918*, p. 42.

[2] One per cent in 1918.

[3] *Statement of the Auditor of Public Accounts*, January 18, 1921.

[4] United States Internal Revenue, *Statistics of Income for 1918*, p. 24.

tax which is collected by the revenue agent costs 20 per cent of the amount collected (the revenue agent's commission) and the remaining 80 per cent is turned over to the state.

2. *Efforts to reform the Mississippi law*

The Mississippi income tax law was regarded as a failure almost from the first and repeated efforts have been made to substitute a more effective measure. The Senate and House Committee on Revenue which reported in 1918 recognized the fact that changes in income tax practice had come about since 1912, and recommended sweeping changes: [1]

The present income tax law of Mississippi should be repealed outright. We recommend the passage of a law with progressive rates, taxing incomes of both individuals and corporations. . . . The law we submit is an adaptation of the Wisconsin and Federal income tax statutes to Mississippi conditions. . . . It is necessary that the State Tax Commission be given administration of the law, and that they should be provided with funds to administer it properly. Its success or failure is solely a matter of administration.

Meanwhile the state tax commission was exposing the defects of the existing tax system and advocating a net income tax to reach business incomes, with the necessary administrative provisions, as a substitute for privilege taxes. [2]

A bill embodying the recommendations of the Joint Committee was introduced in the legislature of 1918, and was passed in the house but defeated in the senate. The state tax commission at once resumed its persevering appeals for the abolition of the existing law, urging that the repeal was desirable even if a better law could not be substituted. [3]

[1] *Joint Report*, pp. 41, 42.

[2] Mississippi Tax Commission, *Report for 1917*, pp. 11, 20.

[3] Mississippi Tax Commission, *Report for 1919*, pp. 31, 32.

The Legislature would do well to substitute an income tax for the privilege tax. It might be well for this to be done by degrees in order that the State will not be denied any needed revenue. A tax on business should be measured by the net amount of the income of the business. . . . The imposition of an income tax along with the ad valorem tax will reach practically all who should contribute funds for the support of the State Government. With the offset of one against the other, there will not be double taxation.

At the same time the commission expressed its criticism of the state privilege taxes and of the methods of taxing personal property. The privilege taxes were described as imposed on business unequally and therefore unjustly. For example, " a lawyer who has a practice of one thousand dollars per annum pays as much as one who has a practice of twenty thousand dollars per annum." The personal property taxes in their turn are in a confused state. The method of taxing money penalizes the honest man; that of taxing deposits has driven large sums into other states, and the burden is borne by land and tangible property. " There are professional men, making enormous incomes, who pay nothing, practically, because they own no tangible property. Their deposits, cash on hand and customer's accounts cannot be found by the Assessor." [1]

In spite of the urgent recommendations of the state tax commission, repeated from year to year, the legislature of 1920 not only failed to change the income tax law of the state, but even increased the taxes on some privileges more than 100 per cent, with an average increase of 40 per cent.[2] The inadequate personal income tax law of 1912 still stands, therefore, along with the unsatisfactory system of privilege and property taxes.

[1] *Ibid.*, p. 32.

[2] *Bulletin of the National Tax Association*, vol. v, no. 9 (June, 1920), p. 271.

Assistance appeared from an unexpected quarter when the supreme court of the state, in a decision announced early in 1921, held that corporations were subject to the tax. Reference was made to a statute defining a " person " (the term used in the income tax law) as including a corporation. Little additional revenue could be expected in the immediate future, however, as the result of this decision. The question of ascertaining income derived within the state was left untouched, and complications seemed certain to arise. Moreover, the allowance of an offset for *ad valorem* taxes paid destroys much of the efficacy of the tax.

The future of the income tax in Mississippi is uncertain for another reason. It is true, as the state tax commission admits in advocating the adoption of a tax law along the newer lines,[1] that the state cannot expect to have the success with an income tax which manufacturing states have had. Mississippi is largely an agricultural state, and the farmer's inability to state his exact income is proverbial. If taxable incomes from agricultural sources are to be arrived at, a competent corps of accountants must be provided. On the other hand, the success of the federal government in taxing incomes of this kind is breaking down much of the scepticism which previously existed. Accounting methods have undoubtedly improved in Mississippi, as elsewhere. The federal government had nearly 20,000 returns from Mississippi in 1918, with a reported net income of more than $70,000,000.[2] If these returns were utilized by the state, as the tax commission has urged, the state income tax could be made far more effective.

[1] *Report for 1919,* p. 32.
[2] United States Internal Revenue, *Statistics of Income for 1918,* pp. 22, 23.

3. *The history of the Oklahoma tax*

The third state to enact important income tax legislation in this period was Oklahoma, which passed a new law in 1915. Oklahoma already had an income tax law of the older type, which had been provided for at the time of the organization of the state government. The constitution adopted in 1907 included a provision for graduated income taxes,[1] and a law imposing a professional income tax was passed almost immediately.[2] According to the terms of this law a graduated tax was laid on all incomes from salaries, fees, professions, and property in excess of $3,500 upon which a gross-receipts or excise tax had not been paid. The law applied to personal incomes only. The rates progressed from one-half of one per cent on incomes from $3,500 to $5,000 to three and one-third per cent on amounts in excess of $100,000.

The income tax law of 1907-1908 was unquestionably a failure. The law was unpopular with the taxpayers, the machinery for enforcement was lacking, and the returns were negligible. In the first four years of its operation the state received less than $5,000 annually in income taxes. After recording the insignificant amounts yielded by the tax during the whole period of its operation, the state auditor urged in 1912 that the law should be thoroughly revised or repealed.[3]

The law has, in my opinion, proven a failure as a revenue producer for the State. . . . No uniformity prevails in making income tax returns — there were as many definitions for the term " gross income " as there were persons examined. . . . This is a

---

[1] *Constitution of the State of Oklahoma*, art. x, sec. 12.

[2] *Laws of Oklahoma*, 1907-08, ch. 81.

[3] *Third Biennial Report of the State Auditor of Oklahoma*, 1912, pp. 235, 236.

chaotic condition and unless the next Legislature deems it advisable to amend the law " in detail " I would recommend that the act be repealed.

After repeated recommendations of this kind had been made, the legislature of 1915 undertook a drastic revision of the whole income tax law.[1] The tax was applied to the entire net income of each and every person in the state and to income from property owned or business carried on in the state by persons residing elsewhere. Deductions for ordinary business expenses, taxes, losses, and bad debts were permitted. The exemptions were $3,000 for the individual $4,000 for husband and wife together, $300 for each child under 18, and $200 for each other dependent. The allowance for a child or dependent became $500 for each child or dependent engaged solely in acquiring an education. The proceeds were assigned to the current expenses of the state government. The administration remained in the hands of the state auditor.

The following schedule of rates was adopted:

Taxable income of individuals	Rate (per cent)
1st $10,000	1
Next $15,000	2
Next $25,000	3
Next $50,000	4
Additional amounts (*i. e.*, above $100,000)	5

In 1917 the rates were decreased and the following schedule was adopted:[2]

Taxable income of individuals	Rate (per cent)
1st $10,000	.75
Next $15,000	1.50
Additional amounts (*i. e.*, above $25,000)	2.00

[1] *Laws of Oklahoma*, 1915, ch. 164.

[2] *Laws of Oklahoma*, 1917, ch. 265.

The law remained in other important respects the same, and is still customarily referred to as the law of 1915.

Increased collections immediately resulted from the changes made in 1915. The tax yielded slightly more than $250,000 for the year 1915 and over $400,000 for the year 1916. The amount yielded for 1916 was greater than the combined collection of the preceding seven-year period.

The collections in 1919 (on 1918 incomes) reached approximately $500,000,[1] or about seven per cent of the state's receipts from taxes for 1918.[2] The cost of collection is probably between two and three per cent of the amount collected.[3]

Oklahoma is obviously one of the poorer states, and large sums from income taxes cannot be expected. Judged only by *relative* standards, however, the state income tax is not a prime source of revenue. Oklahoma is collecting only about one-fifteenth as much as the federal government collects from income taxes in the state,[4] while Wisconsin collects one-seventh as much. The state has continued to exhibit a desire to improve its revenue system, however, and to experiment with new devices; so that the agitation for the revision of the income tax which sprang up again in 1921 may still result in a tax law of the modern type.

The right of the state of Oklahoma to tax the incomes of non-residents has been repeatedly questioned. A decision of the United States Supreme Court rendered March 1,

[1] Oklahoma State Auditor, *Statement*, April 3, 1920.

[2] United States Bureau of the Census, *Financial Statistics of States*, 1918, p. 70.

[3] Estimated from figures furnished by the Oklahoma State Auditor, April 3, 1920.

[4] $7,649,280 in 1918. (United States Internal Revenue, *Statistics of Income for 1918*, p. 24).

1920, established the validity of the Oklahoma law.[1] In the case under consideration, the right of the state to tax the income from the oil properties in Oklahoma of a resident of Illinois was questioned. It was stated by the court that in our system the states have general and except as limited by the federal constitution, complete dominion over all persons, property and business transactions, within their borders. They are not restricted to property taxes nor to any particular form of excises. To debar the state from exacting a share of the gains derived within its borders " is a proposition so wholly inconsistent with fundamental principles as to be refuted by its mere statement." Just as a state may impose general income taxes upon its own citizens and residents, it may levy a duty of like character, and not more onerous in its effect, upon incomes accruing to non-residents from their property or business within the state, or their occupations carried on therein.

The failure of income taxes to become large revenue-producers in such states as Mississippi and Oklahoma is not to be explained wholly by the form of administration, important as that feature has been recognized to be since the inauguration of the Wisconsin system in 1911. In communities which are largely agricultural the collection of large sums will probably always be difficult, for two simple and widely known reasons: the farmer's income is largely in commodities, not money, and he is proverbially unsystematic in account-keeping. A third reason may perhaps be found in the fact that up to the present economic life has been so organized that it is in industry, commerce, and finance, not in the various forms of agriculture, that the

---

[1] Charles B. Shaffer *vs.* Frank C. Carter, State Auditor, and Abner Bruce, Sheriff of Creek County, Oklahoma, U. S. Supreme Court, March 1, 1920, summarized in *Bulletin of the National Tax Association* vol. v, no. 6 (March, 1920), pp. 180-183.

hugest fortunes are made, so that a community which derives its income from the soil is almost always a community of modest incomes.

Even with the necessary qualifications, however, an income tax may be the lesser of two tax evils. The tax on intangible personal property becomes " a penalty on honesty and a premium on dishonesty," in the words of the Mississippi tax commission, even in these non-manufacturing states. The southern states would do well to look more closely into the matter of income taxes suitable for local conditions, for dissatisfaction with the general property tax is increasing throughout the country and this dissatisfaction is no respecter of states.

CHAPTER IV

THE MASSACHUSETTS INCOME TAX

THE income tax law of Massachusetts was passed in 1916, five years after Wisconsin made its epoch-making experiment, and was the first measure which proved in any way comparable to that of the latter state.

1. *The earlier taxation of incomes*

Legislation providing in one form or another for the partial taxation of incomes has been continuously on the statute books of Massachusetts since colonial times, although the early faculty tax in Masssachusetts bore little relation to the modern income tax.[1]

In 1634 there was enacted in the Colony of Massachusetts Bay the first general tax law in any American colony, and included in this act was a provision for the assessment of each man " according to his estate and with the consideration of all other his abilityes whatsoever ". . . . Gradually the faculty tax developed from its original form to an express provision for the taxation of income from a profession, trade, or employment in excess of a given sum. This exemption was fixed at $600 in the act of 1849, raised to $1,000 in 1866, and in 1873, as the result of a compromise with those who were then making an endeavor to have the tax entirely repealed, was changed to $2,000, at which figure it remained until the present income tax act.

In the latter part of the nineteenth century the tax situa-

[1] Massachusetts Tax Commissioner, *Report*, 1917, p. 5.

tion in Massachusetts became serious.[1] The general property tax was becoming less and less satsfactory. In the
period from 1879 to 1900 the tax rates showed heavy increases, and real estate valuations were increased as a result. Tangible personal property was seriously affected,
except where it could escape by incorporation. Intangible
personal property escaped taxation in several ways. It
showed a greater tendency to leave communities in which
tax rates were high and to concentrate in certain residential
towns in which the taxpayers had a high degree of control
over the amount of their assessments. The wealthiest residential towns of the state became more and more favored
in their revenue from personal property and from corporation and bank taxes. According to Professor Bullock "it
is probable that the student of taxation would have difficulty
in finding elsewhere such extreme concentration of taxable
resources as was gradually brought about in Massachusetts
after 1865." [2] In a variety of ways it was possible to evade
the assessment of personal property without a change of
domicile. As a result personal property paid a decreasing
proportion of the local taxes. The percentage which the
personal property assessment formed of the total local
assessments declined from 36.0 in 1850 to 21.8 in 1907.

During this period of continually increasing complications in the tax system of Massachusetts the income tax was
several times under consideration, but it was generally regarded as an isolated survival of an older order, whose usefulness had become questionable, rather than as an immediate and practical remedy for the disease with which
personal property taxation was suffering. In 1870 the in-

[1] C. J. Bullock, "The Taxation of Property and Income in Massachusetts," *Quarterly Journal of Economics* vol. xxxi, no. 1 (Nov. 1916),
pp. 24 *et seq.*

[2] Bullock, *op. cit.*, p. 28.

come tax was brought into the public attention by a court decision that the profits of merchants who employed taxable property in their business were not exempt from taxation as derived from property already taxed although for a number of years previous such property had been considered to be exempt.[1] This decision led to the movement noted above to repeal the tax, and to the resulting compromise of an exemption limit raised to $2,000. In 1875 a special commission on taxation reported that the income tax was assessed in only a few localities and that the revenue yielded was inconsiderable. Enough of a sentiment was found in its favor to prevent a recommendation for repeal, and it seems to have been recognized that even with its imperfections it was of some importance in reaching the ability of persons who were inadequately taxed under the general property tax. It is interesting to note that at this early date a discovery was made which did not reach fruition until another state began afresh more than a quarter of a century later: the Massachusetts committee of 1875 reported that the system suffered by local administration and recommended a "central supervising department of taxes." Unfortunately the recommendation was not followed, and the income tax fell into still greater disrepute. Severe criticism of the injustice and inequality with which the tax operated was expressed by a committee of Boston business men in 1889 and by a committee of the city of Boston in 1891.[2] In 1893 the subject was again taken up by a legislative committee, and the questions of taxing both income and the property from which it was derived and of the local inequalities in the assessment of the tax were again gone over. Once again, however, the committee reported against the repeal of the tax.

[1] Seligman, *op. cit.*, p. 391, *et seq.*

[2] *Ibid.*, pp. 393, 394.

In 1897 the income tax was again investigated by a taxation commission. Figures showing the inadequacy of the assessment of income in comparison with the assessment of personalty in the state were presented, and the possibility of substituting a new general state income tax for the increasingly unsatisfactory property tax was discussed. This commission was composed of able men in the tax field, and it was almost the first to recognize and to express clearly the relationship of the taxation of income to the taxation of property. Nevertheless the commission concluded that the traditions and habits of the country at the time were not such as would facilitate the administration of an income tax and reported against its adoption. For a number of years after this carefully-framed report was rendered the question of the abolition of the old tax and the introduction of a general state income tax received little attention in Massachusetts. The situation with regard to the taxation of personal property was growing steadily worse but interest was centered on minor reforms in the assessment of property taxes rather than on fundamental changes.

The requirements of the law as it stood at this time were briefly as follows:[1]

[Personal estate for the purposes of taxation shall include:] . . . Fourth. The income from an annuity and the excess above $2,000 of the income from a profession, trade or employment accruing to the person to be taxed during the year ending on the first day of April of the year in which the tax is assessed. Income derived from property subject to taxation shall not be taxed.

As the terms of the law indicate, the rate of taxation upon income was not fixed, but was the same as that for other property taxed under the law. Moreover, great freedom of interpretation was given to the local taxing units,

[1] *Laws of Massachusetts*, 1909, ch. 490, part I, sec. 4, as amended.

and so long as the units made up their part of the total state tax there was no pressure upon them to enforce that particular part of the law under which personal incomes were subject to taxation. As a result the scope of the tax was narrow, the returns insignificant and irregular, and the operation of the law unfair and erratic. As late as 1914 a critic comments as follows:[1]

The assessment of salaries and personal incomes has virtually disappeared, except in an occasional instance of a college professor or of a state official, and in the few cases where business incomes are assessed at all, the assessment is added to the personal property tax and does not figure separately on the tax books. What is therefore still called the income tax in Massachusetts is nothing but an equal and entirely arbitrary additional assessment upon a few members of the professional classes and a few large business men selected at haphazard in Boston and one or two other towns.

In 1911 the new point of view with regard to state income taxes which was making itself apparent in Wisconsin in the passage of an income tax law showed itself in Massachusetts in the governor's recommendation to the legislature of the adoption of an income tax. It was plain that opinion everywhere was changing. Such a proposal as that which was made in Massachusetts was probably made possible by the submission to the states of the 16th amendment (providing for a federal income tax). The governor's recommendation met with less opposition than was at first anticipated, but the difficulties of framing a satisfactory income tax law were advanced in many quarters as reasons for prolonging the old system of taxation of personal property. The question of a progressive rate and that of the exemption from taxation of property taxed under the income tax proved particularly troublesome. Meanwhile Wisconsin was furnishing an example of the

[1] Seligman, *op. cit.*, p. 397.

possible use of a state income tax and public opinion was
being molded from within the state by the annual reports
of the state tax commissioner and by various organizations
representing special interests.   In 1914 a constitutional
amendment permitting the levy of a proportional income
tax but not containing a requirement that property taxed
upon its income must be exempted from other taxation
passed both branches of the legislature.   In 1915 the
amendment was again passed by the legislature, and in
November of that year it was ratified by the people.[1]   The
legislature of 1915 had appointed a special commission to
draft an income tax law.   This commission utilized a bill
prepared by the Massachusetts Tax Association which was
in large part the work of Professor Charles J. Bullock of
Harvard University, and after introducing changes which
it considered desirable presented it to the legislature of
1916.   The bill became law in the spring of that year,[2] in
so workable a form that in the succeeding years only
minor amendments have been made.

The Massachusetts income tax law, unlike the Wisconsin
law and the majority of the laws which were subsequently
passed, is not a law applying to all kinds of income.   It
taxes only specified kinds of income, and in order to avoid
double taxation, exempts the classes of income from real
estate, dividends of Massachusetts corporations, income
from savings bank deposits, and interest on mortgages secured by Massachusetts real estate for an amount equal to
the mortgage.   The tax on intangible personal property was
abolished.

[1] *Laws of Massachusetts*, 1916, 44th Amendment to the Constitution,
pp. 50, 53.

[2] *Laws of Massachusetts*, 1916, ch. 269.   (An Act to impose a tax
upon the income received from certain forms of intangible property
and from trades and professions.)

The classification of the incomes taxable, together with
the differing rates, produces a separation of earned and unearned income, with a higher rate of taxation upon the
latter.

The four kinds of income taxed under the Massachusetts
law are as follows:

I. *Income from intangibles,* taxed at *six per cent.*
(For the years 1918 to 1921 inclusive, the rate is six and
one-half per cent).[1] The only exemption is the provision
that persons whose income from all sources is less than
$600 may claim an exemption of $300.

2. *Income from annuities,* taxed at *one and one-half per
cent.* There is a possible exemption of $300, as in the
case of intangibles. (Annuities were formerly taxed
locally at varying rates).

3. *Net gains from dealings in intangibles,* taxed at *three
per cent.* This applies alike to professional dealers in
securities and to speculators and private investors.

4. *Income from professions, employment, trade, or
business,* taxed at *one and one-half per cent.* (For the
yours 1918 and 1919 the rate is two and one-half per cent).[2]
Exemptions are permitted of $2,000 for the individual,
$2,500 for husband and wife, and $250 for each child
under 18 or dependent parent, with a total aside from that
of the original $2,000 for the individual, of not more than
$1,000. In addition to the above taxes, a " war tax " of 10
per cent of the taxes paid was required for the years 1918
and 1919.[3]

The act applies to inhabitants of Massachusetts, to Massachusetts partnerships, to estates of deceased persons, and

[1] *Laws of Massachusetts,* 1919, ch. 342.
[2] *Laws of Massachusetts,* 1919, ch. 324.
[3] *Laws of Massachusetts,* 1918, ch. 252.

to estates held in trust. Taxes upon estates, partnerships, and trustees and other fiduciaries are imposed only to the extent that the income accrues for the benefit of an inhabitant of Massachusetts.

The act itself does not apply directly to corporations, but domestic corporations are subject to a tax of two and one-half per cent, similar to the tax on incomes from professions, employment, trade, or business described above.[1] This tax is called an excise tax on net income.

Massachusetts followed the example of the only state which up to 1916 had made a financial success of an income tax law,—Wisconsin—and centralized the administration. The tax commissioner, who was charged with the administration of the tax, was authorized to appoint an income tax deputy to have general charge of the taxation of incomes. The state was to be divided into districts, with an income tax assessor for each district. Professor Bullock comments as follows upon the type of administration decided upon:[2]

It was not to be expected that the tax would work well if administered in approximately three hundred and fifty ways by approximately three hundred and fifty local boards of assessors; and Massachusetts acted wisely in turning the work over to the Commonwealth. During the fifty years of its existence the tax commissioner's department has been administered in a manner that has commanded general confidence, and all that needed to be done was to add to its equipment a new bureau charged with the assessment and collection of the income tax.

Massachusetts adopted a system of information at the source but which has worked fairly satisfactorily. Every employer was required to report concerning those persons

[1] *Laws of Massachusetts*, 1919, ch. 355.
[2] Bullock, *op. cit.*, p. 57.

to whom more than $1,800 had been paid during the pre-
vious calendar year. Corporations doing business in the
state were also required to report the names of their share-
holders, and others to whom they made payments.

At the time when the terms of the Massachusetts law
were worked out the complications of the problem of dis-
tributing the yield of the income tax were not as clearly
recognized as they are at the present time; but the local
difficulties of assessing the personal property tax had been
so great and so conspicuous that pressure from that direction resulted in a carefully made plan for the use and disposition of the revenue. During the first years of the
operation of the law the local taxing units were reimbursed
according to a carefully worked-out formula for the losses
which they were assumed to have suffered by the elimination of the old tax on intangible personal property. The
balance was then distributed to the cities and towns on the
same basis as the assessment of the state tax. Expenses
of administration were subtracted before the distribution
was made. This scheme was admittedly only temporary,
and in 1919 a scheme was adopted by which a gradually decreasing amount of the proceeds of the income tax should
be distributed in reimbursement for losses from the personal property tax, and a correspondingly increasing
amount should be distributed in proportion to the amount
of the state tax.[1] After 1928 the whole amount of the
revenue from the income tax was to be distributed according to the amount of the state tax assessed. This plan was
interfered with by a law passed shortly after it was
adopted,[2] as a part of the education act. According to the
terms of this law a permanent plan of reimbursement to

[1] *Laws of Massachusetts*, 1919, ch. 314.
[2] *Laws of Massachusetts*, 1919, ch. 363.

the cities and towns for school expenditures was adopted. A scale of partial reimbursements for salaries according to the amounts received by teachers and other educational officials and a second scale of reimbursements graduated according to the ratio of the valuation of real and personal property to net average membership in public day schools, so that the towns with the smallest valuations in proportion to school attendance should receive the largest amount of assistance, were adopted at the same time. About $4,000,000 was distributed in this way, with excellent results as far as the raising of teachers' salaries was concerned. The distribution was regarded as inadequate by the state commissioner of education, and early in 1921 a movement for a distribution of an additional $3,000,000 of the proceeds of the income tax was gathering strength in Massachusetts. The movement was opposed by residents of Boston on the ground that in this way Boston was assessed for the benefit of cities and towns which should bear their own educational burdens, and defended by educational officials and farming interests, who urged that the burdens of the schools upon the cities and towns should be equalized and the work standardized. The difficulties of attaining fair and satisfactory distribution of income tax funds are brought out clearly by the argument in Massachusetts. In this state, as elsewhere, the advantages of a distribution to the localities and the consequent obviousness of the lightening of the tax burden seem in part to be outweighed by the local controversies as to the justice with which the distributon is effected in practice.

The elasticity of the income tax is recognized in Massachusetts as it is in Wisconsin. The legislature of 1919 turned to it for resources with which to meet a temporary financial emergency,—the obligations assumed by the commonwealth towards ex-soldiers—and increased the rate on business incomes by one per cent, and the rate on income from intangibles by one and one-half per cent, as noted above. The legislature of the previous year had ordered an increase of 10 per cent of the taxes paid for the year, thus increasing the yield by $1,237,057.[1] These experiments are not as radical as those made by Wisconsin, which doubled the greater part of the scale of rates, but they are important enough to render the tax unnecessarily unpopular. The purpose of an addition to an existing tax is readily lost sight of, and the tax appears unduly burdensome; while a special tax imposed for such a purpose as that of raising funds to pay a soldier's bonus operates to keep the particular emergency clearly in mind. Changes in the rate of the income tax in order to make the final adjustment between estimates of expenses and receipts ordinarily arise from a situation of another kind,[2] and might prove more satisfactory. Such a policy has been used in Great Britain in determining the rates of the income tax, and might, with a satisfactory budget system, prove feasible in this country.

2. *Financial results in Massachusetts*

The income tax in Massachusetts has been a conspicuous success from a financial point of view. The rates are moderate, except for the income from intangibles, and they include no progressive feature; but the administration is centralized, like that of Wisconsin, and efficiency in collecting the tax was therefore to be expected from the beginning. Moreover, the annual flow of wealth in Massachu-

[1] Massachusetts Tax Commissioner, *Report*, 1918, p. 32.

[2] Lutz, in a *Report on the Operation of State Income Taxes*, presented to the Ohio Special Joint Taxation Committee, September 18, 1919, p. 102, of the Taxation Committee's report, suggests that the Massachusetts experiments prove the feasibility of a flexible adjustment of this kind.

setts is great. Massachusetts ranks as the fourth state in
the order of the amount of personal income taxes paid to
the federal government, and is outranked only by New
York, Pennsylvania, and Illinois.[1] A carefully devised
tax law, efficiently administered, should therefore be a
productive and reliable revenue measure.

The income taxes collected in Massachusetts stand as
follows for the first four years of the operation of the
law:[2]

Year of collection (on incomes of previous year)	Amount collected	Amount distributed
1917	$12,535,630	$12,207,769
1918	14,882,545	14,463,644
1919	15,646,872	15,019,937
1920	16,233,544	15,230,712

Owing to the fact that almost all of the proceeds of the
Massachusetts tax are distributed to the local units, the
fraction which they form of the total state tax receipts
has no particular significance. An idea of the remarkable
success of the Massachusetts income tax may be gained,
however, by noting the fact that if income tax receipts were
added to the total state tax receipts, the income tax receipts
would form roughly one-third of the whole sum.

The Massachusetts tax is preëminently successful when
judged by a second standard. The federal taxes on personal incomes collected in Massachusetts in 1918 were
$81,307,340.[3] Massachusets is obtaining from one-fifth
to one-sixth as much from the state income tax as the
federal government is obtaining, thus outranking even Wisconsin.

[1] United States Internal Revenue, *Statistics of Income for 1918*, p. 24.

[2] Massachusetts Commissioner of Corporations and Taxation, *Report for 1920*, p. 19.

[3] United States Internal Revenue, *Statistics of Income for 1918*, p. 24.

The cost of collection in Massachusetts is remarkably low.   It is reported as follows:[1]

Year	Cost of collection (Per cent of total assessment)
1917	1.86
1918	1.44
1919	2.00
1920	1.80

The rise in the cost for 1919 is partly accounted for by the occupation of new premises.

An analysis of the returns for 1920 shows that the greater part of the revenue is furnished by the tax on intangibles.   The proportions furnished from the various sources are as follows:[2]

Source	Per cent of total tax (including additional 1 and ½ per cent)
Business income	40.69
Annuities	.14
Gains	5.66
Interest and dividends	53.51

3. *The success of the income tax*

The Massachusetts income tax has proved to be more productive and less disturbing to individual taxpayers than even its advocates expected.   The *yield* has more than justified the anticipations of those who prophesied large additions to the tax revenues from this source.   The tax is *elastic,* as is shown by the large income promptly obtained from the special " war taxes " and from the temporary taxes added soon afterwards.   Its *cost of collection* is low.

[1] Massachusetts Tax Commissioner, *Report*, 1917, p. 15; 1918, p. 27; 1919, p. 40; 1920, p. 16.

[2] Massachusetts Commissioner of Corporations and Taxation, *Report for 1920*, p. 15.

The tax has produced a more *equitable* system by increasing the revenue from intangibles. It has effected a better *distribution* of the tax burden among the various communities of the state. The tax commissioner in 1917 emphasized the improvement in bookkeeping by individuals and associations engaged in business, and noted a slighter tendency than that which existed before the passage of the act for individuals to leave the state in order to escape taxation. A consideration which is fully as important as any of these is to be found (in the state of public opinion,) in the general impression that taxation in the state is less unjust and unequal than previously.[1]

There is a general feeling of satisfaction by the change to an income tax which we find expressed by all classes of people. The wealthier class, in most cases, are paying more than in the past; many who never paid in previous years are now bearing their share of the tax burden; and many of small means, by the exemption provided by the act, are now given proper relief.

The tax commissioner in 1919 again noted an improvement in bookkeeping methods throughout the state. The improvement has been noticeable in each year, as modern bookkeeping and accounting systems are installed as a result of the division audits. The steady improvement not only facilitates the assessment and collection of the income tax, but has an effect upon the conduct of business generally. One of the necessary results is the elimination of the majority of the bankruptcy cases which are to be traced to an ignorance of the internal affairs of the business.

With regard to the general opinion as to the justice of taxing incomes, the commissioner reported in 1919 as follows:[2]

[1] Massachusetts Tax Commissioner, *Report,* 1917, p. 19.
[2] *Report,* 1919, pp. 42, 43.

There seems to be no abatement of the general satisfaction with this method of taxation, not a single taxpayer having been met with who wishes to return to the general property tax system. The burden of governmental maintenance is more equitably distributed than ever before.   There is a noticeable reaction from abnormal centralization of wealth in favored localities—a condition alarmingly prevalent before the Income Tax Law came into operation.

After having observed the effects of the increased rates voted in 1919 for the purpose of raising funds for a soldiers' bonus, the tax commissioner gave warning against the further extension of the rates.   In his opinion additional increases in the rates would inevitably result in loss of revenue through the disturbing effect on the investor. In the course of the year (1919) several cases of change of domicile had occurred, in sufficiently important instances to have come to the attention of the income tax divisions, which had been attributed to the constantly increasing rates.   At the close of the year the situation did not appear serious, but it gave a significant warning for the future.

The classification of the various kinds of income, a matter which seemed very simple when the income tax law was devised, is now proving troublesome.   The tax commissioner comments on this situation as follows: [1]

Possibly the one criticism of our income tax system which can be made with some semblance of justification lies in the complications incident to the various classifications of taxable and exempt income.   While, fundamentally, these classifications, or most of them, rest upon perfectly sound foundations, yet it is still an undeniable fact that the complexities incident to the four classifications as established are somewhat of a handicap both to the administration of the law and to the tax-paying public, who find it quite difficult properly to allocate the various kinds of income in their returns.   In the course of approximately 8,000 verifications

[1] *Report*, 1919, pp. 13, 14.

of returns made within the past two years, nearly half that number were found to be in error, either in favor of or against the interests of the taxpayer.

The first step towards simplifying the classification is suggested by the tax commissioner as that of abolishing the group of "net gains from dealing in intangibles," taxed at three per cent, and including this income in the business classification. This part of the tax formed only 1.38 per cent of the total taxes on income returned in 1919, while business income formed 35.03 per cent of the total, and its inclusion with the latter tax seems a simplification through which little administrative or financial value would be lost.

The Massachusetts law provides for the exemptions for minor children only up to the age of 18. This age is below that at which young persons in the colleges and universities can become self-supporting, and frequent complaints as to its injustice are heard:[1]

Is the present age limit a just and fair one to the average taxpayer? When it is considered that as time goes on more and more of our young men and women are seeking higher education, not alone from the homes of the wealthy but from the homes of mechanics and the great middle classes (so called) as well as those of moderately circumstanced merchants and relatively low-salaried professional men; when it is realized that many a parent of moderate though taxable income is financing one or more boys or girls through a college course; and, particularly, when it is acknowledged that between the ages of eighteen and twenty-one years the expense of maintenance of dependent children, especially the child in college, is more than double the expense of any prior year,—there seems to be much equity in the frequent complaint that the age-limit of eighteen years is too low and that this limit may well be raised to twenty-one years, the legal and generally recognized age of independence.

In addition to changes in the classification of incomes,

[1] *Report,* 1919, p. 15.

and an extension of the age of dependent children for which an exemption is allowed, the Massachusetts authorities are urging reforms which will effect the personnel of the income tax administration. It is urged that the Massachusetts employees should be placed under a suitable competitive civil-service rating, and that the salaries offered should be made more nearly commensurate with those offered for similar degrees of ability in private enterprises.

4. *Present income tax problems in Massachusetts*

If it is carefully handled and if the legislature refrains from tampering with it on occasions of temporary financial pressure, the Massachusetts income tax will probably prove to be a stable, reliable, and productive source of revenue, collected with as little dissatisfaction as any tax is likely to be collected with. The dangers of utilizing the income tax to meet sudden financial emergencies have already been discussed. The reports of the Massachusetts tax commissioner indicate that in some quarters at least they are realized in Massachusetts, and it is probable that after the period of collecting the funds for soldier's bonuses has passed the state will not again rely upon such extensions of the tax, at least for some time to come.

As far as the form of the law is concerned, the chief differences of the Massachusetts income tax law from the income tax laws of the two other states which are most important in this field, Wisconsin and New York, are those of its selection of four types of income for taxation and of the imposition of a proportional rate. It is inevitable that a change of plan in Massachusetts should come up for discussion soon, particularly if the New York law proves to work smoothly. The actual effect of the Massachusetts plan is that of *differentiating* four different kinds of personal income, imposing different rates upon the different

classes, and so fixing these rates that investment or "unearned" income is taxed at an unusually high rate, proportional in character. The proportional rate itself is probably not one of the most serious parts of the problem. The
best of modern expert tax opinion is in favor of state income tax rates which, if progressive, reach only a low
maximum; and it is an open question whether the arguments for such a scale, such as the one-two-three-per cent
scale employed in New York, are more convincing than the
arguments for a simple proportional tax, possibly a two
per cent tax, upon personal incomes. With the federal income tax scale as an ever-present background for the state
taxes on personal incomes, the scope of the state rates must
always be limited. Differentiation of types of income is a
more involved problem. A plan of differentiation adopted
later than the Massachusetts plan, that of North Dakota's
income tax system of 1919, proved to be unworkable.
Meanwhile Massachusetts, a much richer state, found this
sources of income the most productive of the four sources
tapped by the income tax act, and relied upon it for more
than one-half of the state income tax receipts. Surpris-
ingly, this heavy tax upon funded incomes failed to arouse
any unusual dissatisfaction. With the development of the
personal income tax in the adjacent state of New York,
and the imposition of a more moderate rate upon investment income, this state of affairs in Massachusetts may become less placid.

Another unusual factor in Massachusetts is the exemption from taxation under the personal income tax of income from real estate. Historically this is easily explic-
able, and the traditional aversion to taxing both income and
the source from which it is derived is well known. In the
course of the present period of development of state income taxes, however, there has come to be less and less dis-

cussion of means in which double taxation of this kind may be avoided, and more of an effort to devise simple plans by which tax burdens may be adjusted equitably among the individuals affected. The exemption of the income from investment in Massachusetts corporations is another illustration of the complicated arrangement into which Massachusetts entered, working under the older idea that double taxation of income must be avoided at any cost. The extension of the Massachusetts taxes on occupational income and on investments to income *from whatever source and wherever derived* would simplify the law, diminish popular confusion as to the reasons for the various exemptions, and (if accompanied by a corresponding reduction in the rate of tax on investment income) results simply in heavier taxation of the sources from which funded incomes are derived.

CHAPTER V

INCOME TAXES IN MISSOURI AND DELAWARE

1. *The Missouri income tax*

IN 1917, the year following the passage of the new Massachusetts law, the states of Missouri and Delaware, both relatively inexperienced in this form of taxation, undertook to tax personal incomes.

Missouri had had an income tax of short duration as a Civil War measure, but had given it up almost immediately after the close of the war, and had tried no tax of the kind since that time. The law passed in 1917 therefore marked a new and important step in the fiscal history of the state.[1]

The new law imposed a tax of one-half of one per cent on incomes from all sources derived within the state. It applied to individuals and corporations. Incomes of single persons to the amount of $3,000 and of heads of families to the amount of $4,000 were exempt. Deductions for business expenses, interest, taxes, losses, bad debts, and depreciation were permitted. Receipts for state taxes on property were acceptable in payment of income taxes. The state auditor was given supervision of the tax, and the regular assessors and collectors of the counties became also assessors and collectors of the income tax. The proceeds apparently were intended to go to the state. This tax was first collected in 1918, on incomes received in the latter half

[1] *Laws of Missouri*, 1917, pp. 524-538.

of 1917.   In the same year the law was declared constitutional by the Missouri Supreme Court.[1]

An income tax on this modest scale was inadequate for
the financial needs of the state, a fact which was recognized
by the legislators of the following year.   In 1919 a consistent attempt was made to increase the state revenue from
various sources.   The income tax law was amended, and
the rate increased from one-half of one per cent to one and
one-half per cent.[2]   The exemptions were reduced from
$4,000 for heads of families and $3,000 for others to
$2,000 and $1,000 respectively.   Provision was made for
an additional exemption of $200 for each dependent child.
An important change was contained in the repeal of the
section of the law of 1917 which permitted the presentation of receipts for state property taxes in payment of income taxes.   As a result the Missouri income tax became
an addition to the tax system of the state rather than a
substitute for the property tax.   In 1921 the rate was reduced to one per cent.

The amounts collected on incomes are as follows:[3]

Year of collection	Amount collected
1918 } 1919 }	$686,785
1920	2,762,171

The tax collected in 1920 had been expected to yield
nearly double the amount recorded, as the total amount of
taxes charged under the assessment was $4,623,374.   The
diminished collections were caused by a decision of the
Supreme Court sustaining the contention that the increased
taxes must be paid only on the income of that part of the

[1] Glasgow *vs.* Rowse, 43 Mo. l. c, 489, 490, 491.

[2] *Laws of Missouri*, 1919, Act of May 6th.

[3] Missouri State Auditor, *Statements*, March 19, 1920, Dec. 21, 1920.

year succeeding the passage of the new (1919) law. The
incomes of 1920 are expected to yield from $4,000,000 to
$4,500,000 in income taxes.

The assessments of individuals on 1919 incomes formed
almost one-half of the total assessment. On the asump-
tion that collections are divided in the same way, individual
incomes contributed $1,203,000, or about one-seventeenth
of the amount collected by the federal government on 1918
incomes.

The receipts from the income tax for the year 1918
formed slightly more than eight per cent of the total tax
receipts of the state. For the year 1919 the income tax
receipts formed twenty-six per cent of the total tax receipts.[1] The costs are not separated from those for making the general assessment of property.

In spite of the efforts of the legislature of 1919 to reform the law, it remains inadequate. An act which imposes so low a rate, lacks the feature of graduation, and
provides for no separate central or local administration, has
not reached its maximum of productiveness. Comparisons
with the Wisconsin income tax are hardly valid, however;
for although Missouri is the richer state, as the returns to
the federal government for the personal net incomes of the
last three years show,[2] its governmental expenses are con-
siderably less,[3] and it is unnecessary to attempt to raise as
large amounts by taxation. Moreover, the number of individual returns in Missouri in 1919 (95,956)[4] is not far

[1] United States Bureau of the Census, *Financial Statistics of States,*
1918, p. 70; 1919, p. 64.

[2] United States Internal Revenue, *Statistics of Income for 1918,* pp.
32, 33.

[3] United States Bureau of the Census, *Financial Statistics of States,*
1918, p. 80; 1919, p. 74.

[4] Missouri State Auditor, *Statement,* Dec. 21, 1920.

behind the federal government's number from Missouri for 1918, (110,890) when the personal exemptions stood at the same figures. As Missouri's governmental expenses rise, it may be necessary to revise the law along the lines of the Wisconsin legislation.

2. *The Delaware income tax*

Before 1917 Delaware had levied taxes for only two brief periods. A faculty tax was adopted in 1796, to be assessed proportionately to the " gains and profits " of merchants, tradesmen, mechanics, and manufacturers, but it soon feel into disuse. Just after the close of the Civil war a tax was imposed on salaries and fees, but it was succeeded by a license tax in 1871.[1]

The personal income tax law passed in Delaware in 1917 was more promising than that of Missouri, passed in the same year, in that it imposed a higher rate (one per cent) and allowed smaller deductions.[2] On the other hand, the tax was not applied to corporations or to non-residents. Persons with incomes of not more than $1,000 were exempt. Business expenses, interest on indebtedness, taxes, losses, bad debts, and depreciation allowances were to be deducted. A striking feature was the exclusion of gains from agricultural operations. The state treasurer, assisted by an income tax clerk and a special collector of state revenue, was charged with the administration of the law. It was assumed that the state treasury was to receive the proceeds of the tax.

In 1919 the law received important amendments.[3] Agricultural gains were brought under the law. The personal exemptions were changed to correspond with those

---

[1] Seligman, *op. cit.*, pp. 378, 379; Kennan, *op. cit.*, p. 212.

[2] *Laws of Delaware*, 1917, ch. 26.

[3] *Laws of Delaware*, 1919, ch. 30.

permitted under the federal law. Two special collectors of state revenue were authorized instead of one, and these collectors were given more extensive power and authority over the methods of collecting the income tax. Proposals for further amendments along the lines of the model income tax law were placed before the legislature of 1921.

The Delaware law has been attacked on the ground that it is in violation of provisions of both federal and state constitutions, but it has successfully withstood the attacks.[1]

The yield of the Delaware income tax stands as follows for the first two years:[2]

Year of collection	Yield
1918	$400,000
1919	317,004

The proceeds of the income tax in Delaware are treated as an addition to the total revenue rather than as a substitute for the revenues formerly derived from unsatisfactory tax measures, as has been so often the case in other states. The greater part of the revenue, $250,000, in each year has been placed to the credit of the school fund. The balance is transferred to the state highway department. The sums available in each year have enabled the schools to have a decided increase and have greatly facilitated the work of the state highway department.

Only that part of the proceeds which are transferred to the state highway department appear as receipts included in the general fund of the state. If that part which is assigned to the state school department is added, the share of the income tax in the receipts of the state treasurer for the two years is as follows:

[1] *Bulletin of the National Tax Association*, vol. v, no. 3 (Dec., 1919), pp. 86, 87.

[2] Delaware State Treasurer, *Report*, 1918, p. 6; *Report*, 1919, p. 6.

Year of collection	Cash receipts of the general fund plus income taxes [1]	Income tax receipts (per cent of total receipts)
1918	$1,678,849	23.8
1919	3,509,722	9.0

The tax collected on incomes received in 1918 was about one-twenty-third of the amount collected by the federal government on personal incomes in Delaware for that year.[2] The cost of collection for the state government was about three per cent.

The system of distribution adopted in Delaware has been commended as one which has the advantages of reasonableness, popularity, and attractiveness to the general public.[3] The use of the whole or a major part of the proceeds of the state income tax for educational purposes readily absorbs the yield of the income tax. A measure for the distribution is available in the school enrollment, and the definite reflection in the individual's tax bill of a reduction in the largest item is calculated to affect the taxpayer's attitude towards the tax.

In Delaware the distribution of the amount of $250,000 which is annually set aside for the use of the schools is made as state aid to elementary schools. The funds are distributed by the trustee of the school fund upon certificate of the state board of education. The schools which conform to the regulations of the board of education are certified by districts, and the trustee of the school fund apportions the amount available to the various districts on the basis of the total elementary school enrollment during

---

[1] Delaware State Treasurer, *Report*, 1918, p. 5; 1919, p. 5.

[2] United States Internal Revenue, *Statistics of Income for 1918*, p. 24.

[3] A. E. Holcomb, " State Income Taxes . . . Methods Employed in Delaware," *Bulletin of the National Tax Association*, vol. vi, no. 4 (Jan. 1921), pp. 126-128.

the preceding year. The enrollment of high schools is left out of account.

A chapter of local political history has an unforeseen effect upon the distribution of the income tax to the schools.[1] The city of Wilmington, which elected not to come under the new school code adopted in 1917, is thereby excluded from the districts which receive state aid, although the city contributes 95 per cent of the income taxes collected.

Neither the decreased collections from the state income tax in the second year of its operation nor the small ratio which the state receipts from the tax bear to the federal collections appear to be considered grounds for expanding the scope of the state income tax. From the beginning the tax has been treated as a means a meant of supplementing the state revenues with a high degree of facility. The yield of the first year established the fact that the tax was adequate for the purposes for which it was used, and the changes made subsequently were for the purpose of rendering the act more equitable in its operation rather than with a view of expanding the revenue from that source.

[1] Holcomb, *op. cit.*, p. 127.

CHAPTER VI

INCOME TAXES IN VIRGINIA, SOUTH CAROLINA, AND NORTH CAROLINA

1. *History of the Virginia income tax*

THE income tax law of Virginia, which has been revised by nearly every legislature of recent years, was given the principal outlines of its present form in 1918.[1] Virginia had made use of the income tax in one or another of its various forms for a longer period than any other state in which the tax is now in force, with the single exception of Massachusetts. Up to 1911 Virginia was regarded as exceptionally successful in its use of this source of revenue, in that the annual proceeds had come to exceed $100,000. The recent revisions in Virginia, with the exception of the inclusion of corporations in 1916, have failed to make essential changes in the law or to bring it in line with the income taxes of the last decade which are so framed as to produce revenues running into the millions.

Virginia maintained the early faculty taxes for only a brief period (1777-1782; 1786-1790).[2] The real beginning of income taxation in the state is to be found in 1843. Since that year an income tax law has remained continuously on the statute books. The law of 1843 laid a tax upon salaries and professional incomes. It was several

[1] *Laws of Virginia*, 1918, ch. 219.
[2] D. O. Kinsman, *The Income Tax in the Commonwealths of the United States* (New York, 1903), pp. 13, 14.

times modified, but it underwent no radical revision until the Civil War period, when thes rates were increased and the classifications changed. After the close of the Civil War the rates were greatly reduced. In 1874 the rate was fixed at one per cent, at which point it remained, up to 1919, and the exemption at $600, where it remained until 1908 when it was raised to $1,000.[1] In 1910 the exemption was raised to $2,000, and in 1916 lowered to $1,200. In 1916 the law was extended to include the income of corporations.[2] In 1919 the rate for incomes in excess of $3,000 was made two per cent.[3]

According to the law now in force[4] a tax of one per cent is imposed on the income of every person or corporation residing or doing business in Virginia up to $3,000, and two per cent on income in excess of that amount. The customary deductions are provided for. The exemptions stand at $1,200 for the individual income, $1,800 for husband and wife together, and $200 for each person entirely dependent and actually supported by the taxpayer. The administration is in the hands of the auditor of public accounts and the county commissioners of the revenue .The receipts are applied to the expenses of the state government.

2. *The yield of the tax in Virginia*

Until corporations were brought under the tax in 1916 the income tax in Virginia produced only a small amount of revenue. Beginning in that year the receipts have

[1] E. Sydenstricker, *A Brief History of Taxation in Virginia* (Richmond, 1915), p. 52.

[2] *Laws of Virginia*, 1916, ch. 472.

[3] *Laws of Virginia*, 1919, ch. 43.

[4] *Laws of Virginia*, 1918, ch. 219, as amended.

greatly increased.   A summary for recent years is as follows:[1]

Year of collection	Receipts from income taxes
1908	$122,058
1909	102,810
1910	106,909
1911	129,429
1912	102,678
1917	353,756
1918	660,745
1919	906,733
1920	1,811,786

The cost of collection ordinarily constitutes slightly less than four per cent of the amount collected.

Although Virginia is still receiving only a comparatively small sum from the income tax on individuals and corporations, the state's whole scale of expenditure is lower than that of the other states previously discussed, with the exception of Delaware and Mississippi.[2]   In 1919 about seven per cent of the total treasury receipts were made up of income taxes.   This percentage was expected to be somewhat larger for the fiscal year ending September 30, 1920.   It is not possible to separate personal from corporate income taxes in the Virginia accounts, so that the exact place of the personal income tax in the Virginia tax system cannot be estimated.

For a number of years preceding the entrance of the United States into the war and the consequent readjustment of financial affairs, public as well as private, the revenue system of Virginia was considered to be in an excep-

---

[1] Sydenstricker, *op. cit.*, p. 53; Virginia Auditor of Public Accounts, *Report*, 1919, p. 6; *statements.*

[2] United States Bureau of the Census, *Financial Statistics of States,* 1919, p. 29.

tionally satisfactory condition. In 1917 the auditor of public accounts stated that in his opinion the financial condition of the state was so fortunate that the rates of taxation on intangible personalty could be reduced and the taxes on tangible personalty entirely removed.[1] These recommendations were made solely on the grounds noted above, namely the presence of a surplus; for the usual dissatisfaction with the operation of the tax on intangibles was conspicuously absent in Virginia at that time.

The recommendations for reductions in the rate of taxation were not followed, and the situation changed so rapidly that in 1919 it was decided that it was necessary to extend the income tax for the purpose of raising additional revenue. Even with the additional rate the income from the tax is still moderate. It should be borne in mind in estimating Virginia's success with the tax that the financial needs of the state are also moderate. On the whole it umust now be granted that Virginia has used the tax satisfactorily, in spite of the absence of centralized administration and other modern provisions.

3. The repeal of the South Carolina income tax law

The only recent example of the failure of an income tax law in such a way that the abandonment of the whole system became necessary was given in South Carolina in 1918.[2] In so far as the failure of the law can be ascribed to any one cause, it appears to lie in the fact that the administration was left in the hands of the local assessors, and accordingly the law was never fully enforced.

---

[1] Virginia Auditor of Public Accounts, *Report*, 1917, pp. xiii, xiv.

[2] *Laws of South Carolina*, 1918. no. 433. An Act to Repeal Sections 354 and 360, Inclusive, of the Code of Laws of 1912, Volume I, Relative to Tax on Incomes and All Acts Amendatory Thereof. Approved Feb. 14, 1918.

The forerunner of the recent income tax law in South Carolina is to be found in colonial times. A law imposing a " faculty tax," passed in 1701, continued in force, with modifications, until the Civil War brought the necessity for additional revenue.[1] During the Civil War a one per cent tax was laid on incomes and certain profits, but this method of taxation proved unpopular and soon after the war it was abandoned. The revival of the tax occurred in 1897, when an income tax on a progressive scale was introduced.[2] It was this law which with few changes remained in operation until the repeal in 1918.

The tax introduced in 1897 was a general income tax, imposed at the following rates:

Income	*Rate (per cent)*
$2,500 but less than $5,000	1
5,000 " " " 7,500	1½
7,500 " " " 15,000	2
15,000 and over	3

The tax applied to the income of persons living outside the state who owned property or conducted business within the state. The word income was to mean " gross profits," and from this amount business expenses were allowed to be deducted in computing net income. The tax was assessed and collected by the same officials and at the same time as other taxes. The proceeds of the tax were to be distributed among the counties according to an apportionment made by the legislature.

The yield of the tax throughout its history was as follows:[3]

[1] Seligman, *op. cit.*, pp. 379, 398.

[2] *Laws of South Carolina*, 1897, ch. 22.

[3] Kennan, *op. cit.*, p. 230; Seligman, *op. cit.*, p. 417; South Carolina Tax Commission, *Report*, 1917, p. 105.

Year	Yield of income tax
1898	$689
1899	4,829
1900	975
1901	609
1902	292
1903	1,476
1904	1,281
1905	2,130
1906	12,201
1907	10,687
1908	8,431
1909	16,236
1911	14,387
1913	17,400
1914	15,303
1915	31,126
1916	27,690
1917	34,050

The tax officials of the state, realizing the impossibility of enforcing the law, have argued its repeal from the beginning. The comptroller general repeatedly described the difficulties of enforcement and concurred in an appeal for the abolition of the law.[1] The state tax commission from the time of its organization expressed great dissatisfaction with the working of the income tax.[2]

This tax, which is most equitable and fair, . . . is unevenly enforced throughout the State. In some counties its enforcement is but partial. . . . We ask the members and other taxpayers to examine the lists in their own counties, and note the absence of names of those whom they know to be liable. . . . The auditors refusing to enforce the law should be removed by the Governor.

In later years the commission became even more explicit in its denunciation of continual lack of enforcement.[3]

[1] Seligman, *op. cit.*, p. 417.
[2] South Carolina Tax Commission, *First Annual Report*, 1915, p. 26.
[3] *Report*, 1916, p. 20.

In some counties but little is done to enforce the law, notably in Darlington, Saluda, and Marlboro. No one appears to pay the tax in these counties. One taxpayer paid in Saluda last year and he quit this year.

With the type of local administration referred to the failure of the law was inevitable. It was a matter of general information throughout the state, almost from the beginning, that there was insufficient provision for the enforcement of the law with the result that a few persons paid an income tax while the vast majority escaped. The repeal of the law in 1918 cleared the revenue code of a tax law the returns of which in recent years had hardly paid for the trouble and expense of collection, and which probably had a demoralizing effect both upon the taxpayers and the assessors.

The income tax in South Carolina was not yet dead, however. The Special Joint Taxation Committee which reported to the legislature in 1921 devoted a considerable amount of attention to the inequitable operation of the general property tax, and the resulting heavy burdens on the farmer. In the same report the argument that taxation of income from property already taxed constitutes double taxation was attacked. The Committee stated that in its opinion the state taxation of incomes relieves property taxed upon an *ad valorem* basis from a part of the double burden of state and local taxation, and leaves the major part of the property tax to one taxing jurisdiction, that of the locality. This, in the opinion of the Committee, " is the place, object, and function of an income tax in a system of state taxation." [1] Although an income tax bill and a business tax bill failed of passage in the legislature of 1921, the determined advocacy of an income tax as a

[1] Quoted in *Bulletin of the National Tax Association*, vol. vi, no. 6 (March, 1921), p. 180.

source of state revenue indicates that the tax is still to be heard from in South Carolina.

4. The taxation of incomes in North Carolina

In 1921 the state of North Carolina completed 72 continuous years of income taxation, and demonstrated its reliance upon this form of tax by the passage of a new law along modern lines.

An income tax was first introduced in North Carolina in 1849, when a three per cent tax was laid upon profits from financial dealings, and a three-dollar tax upon salaries and fees.[1]   The law underwent frequent changes, one of the most important of which was an extension during the Civil War period, when rates were increased and progressive scales introduced.   In 1870 the rate of taxation was greatly reduced.   In succeeding years changes have been made repeatedly.   Another trial of progressive rates was made from 1893 to 1901, but the proportional plan of taxation was reintroduced in the latter year, to be succeeded by a graduated tax in 1919.

According to the law in force in the early years of the present century, a tax of one per cent was imposed upon the excess over $1,000 of gross incomes from all property not otherwise taxed, salaries and fees, annuities, and trades and professions.   The amount yielded by the tax in this form was insignificant, although the receipts had improved over those of earlier years.   In the decade 1890-1900 the revenue from the income tax had ranged from about $2,000 to $4,500 a year.   In the next decade the receipts increased, and furnished from $20,000 to $40,000 a year.   In succeeding years the proceeds expanded as follows:[2]

[1] Seligman, *op. cit.*, p. 403, *et seq.*

[2] North Carolina Tax Commission, *Report*, 1918, p. 20.

Year of collection	*Revenue receipts from income taxes*
1912	$36,497
1913	42,657
1914	50,798
1915	58,606
1916	61,386
1917	64,152
1918	109,285

Although the receipts were steadily expanding during these years, the one per cent rate on personal incomes from specified sources came to be considered inadequate. In 1918 the state tax commission and the corporation commission strongly advocated a constitutional amendment permitting the extension of the law to income from all sources. The program carried through by the General Assembly of 1919 was, however, merely a revision of the rates, by which they were increased and made progressive.

According to the law of 1919 $1,000 of the individual's income, $1,500 for husband and wife together, and an equal amount to widowed persons with minor children, were exempted. The rates of taxation were as follows:

Income	*Rate (per cent)*
Excess above exemption up to $2,500	1
Excess above $2,500 up to $5,000	1½
Excess above $5,000 up to $10,000	2
Excess above $10,000	2½

The changes made in the law of 1919 were far less sweeping than those advocated by the tax officials of the state. Except for the introduction of the progressive scale given above, the new law included no provisions calculated to put the state into line with those which tax incomes from all sources and secure the enforcement of the law through specially appointed income tax officials controlled through a central administrative bureau. The result of adhering to the principle of refusing to tax incomes from property already taxed was great injustice among different classes and occupations. For example, members of the professions were heavily taxed while richer men are almost untouched by the general property tax. It also became apparent that in the period of war expansion " prosperity went untaxed."

An amendment to the constitution was repeatedly and almost continuously urged in North Carolina, and in 1920, in an extra session of the legislature, the amendment was taken under consideration. It was first necessary to remove the constitutional requirement that no income should be taxed when the property from which it is derived is taxed. This was done, and a provision authorizing a maximum rate of six per cent and specified exemptions of $1,000 and $2,000 was favorably acted upon.[1] The amendment was adopted by the people in the election of November, 1920, and preparation was immediately made for the introduction of a new and carefully framed measure in the legislature of 1921.

In estimating the significance of income taxes in this group of states the types of incomes derived within the states should be taken into consideration. In American fiscal history of recent years it seems to be an axiom that income taxation cannot reach a high state of development until intangible personal property has accumulated to such an extent that attempts to evade its taxation have become serious. Obviously this change takes place more slowly in the states in which corporate enterprise—which is often nearly synonymous with manufacturing enterprise—is late in developing. It is not necessarily true that the difficulties with intangibles mean the speedy introduction of taxes on

[1] *Laws of North Carolina* (Special Session), 1920, ch. 5.

personal incomes, as the late entrance of the state of New York into the income tax field proves; but up to the present, at least, the generalization holds good,—that without a dissatisfaction with the taxation of intangible personal property income taxes are neglected or only half-heartedly utilized. The growth of manufacturing in the South and the persevering efforts of each of this group of states to reshape the income tax to suit changing needs have an intricate relationship.

CHAPTER VII

THE NEW YORK INCOME TAX

1. *The history of the movement*

THE fiscal system of the state of New York has undoubtedly had a more careful scrutiny than that of any other state, on account of the magnitude of the state's business and the availability of financial experts of varied interests and of all shades of political opinion. Nevertheless it was not until 1919 that a personal income tax law was passed, and then only after a most detailed and careful study of the possibilities of this form of taxation and of the methods by which it could be adapted to the needs of the state of New York. As the history of taxation in New York state is reviewed, it becomes apparent that all signposts were pointing towards the personal income tax long before public opinion was completely ready for the new measure and before the minor details of the system could be fully worked out.

New York had no share in the early efforts to reach taxpaying ability through the imposition of faculty taxes and no share in the revivals of income taxes in the forties and during the Civil War. For years the mainstay of the state, like that of many of the American states, was the general property tax. As in the neighboring state of Massachusetts, it was not until the country began to taste the post-Civil-War prosperity, and the forms of personal property began to develop, that the evidence of the unworkability of

the general property tax began to accumulate.[1]   The taxation of personal property became increasingly difficult at
a time when state expenditures were rapidly increasing in
amount.   A commission was appointed to investigate the
subject of taxation, but the resulting suggestion of the abolition of the tax on personal property, made in 1871 and
1872, was two generations ahead of its time, and it was
not adopted. Action was necessary, however.   From
1880 until the present the tax system of New York has
been changed and changed again, in the effort to adapt it to
the changing industrial and commercial situation of the
state.   Hardly more than two or three years have passed,
from that date to this, without an experimental change in
the state revenue system.   In 1880 a corporation tax, based
in part upon gross receipts, made its appearance.   From
1885 the influence of an effort to obtain separation of
source is seen in the tax measures adopted.   In that year
a collateral inheritance tax was adopted.   In the following year a new corporation tax, the " organization " tax,
was added.   In 1890 the collateral inheritance tax became
a direct inheritance tax.   In the nineties the movement to
aboish or to minimize the state direct tax gained additional
strength.   Various new taxes were added in that and the
next decade, with so great an increase of revenue from
other sources that the state direct tax played almost no
part in the state revenue system from that year until 1912.
In the course of these years of experimentation many ad-
mirable changes were made and fruitful sources of revenue
were tapped, but the old prime difficulty, that of the under-
assessment and the inequality of assessment of personal
property was hardly touched.   Professor Seligman, who
followed the situation from the early eighties and who

[1] E. R. A. Seligman, " The New York Income Tax," *Political Science
Quarterly*, vol. xxxiv, no. 4 (Dec. 1919), p. 521.

was influential in bringing about the passage of several
of the new measures, describes the situation after 1912 as
follows:[1]

Personal property had almost entirely disappeared from the assessment lists, so that the local tax had become virtually a tax on
real estate.   As the local expenses increased by leaps and bounds
and as the base of taxation was gradually narrowed instead of
broadened, the tax rate began to climb to alarming figures.   The
real-estate interests now clamored for relief; and the public at
large, which realized that the tax on buildings at least was shifted
to them in the shape of increased rent, seconded the effort of the
real-estate owners.

In 1915 two committees were at work on the problem of
taxation in the state of New York: the Joint Legislative
Committee on Taxation, known as the " Mills Committee "
on account of the fact that Senator Mills was at its head,
and the Committee on Taxation of the City of New York,
appointed by Mayor Mitchel and known as the " Mayor's
Committee."   Two main problems were handled,—the
raising of new and additional revenue for the state, and the
just and equitable distribution of the tax burden.   The two
committees worked in close coöperation, realizing the necessity for the most effective action in view of the seriousness
of the tax situation.   The Mayor's Committee, upon which
Professor Seligman was serving as chairman of its execu-
tive committee, studied extensively a single-tax plan of
taxation and a classified property tax, but came to the conclusion that neither was adapted to the needs of New York,
and turned to the income tax.   In the meantime the Mills
Committee had obtained the assistance of Professor H. A.
E. Chandler of Columbia University, who took a large
part in the drafting of its final report, and another drift

[1] Seligman, *op. cit.*, p. 525.

of opinion in the direction of a state income tax was incorporated in this committee's report.   The situation with regard to the state income tax was manifestly changing with great rapidity from year to year.   The federal income tax of 1913 had demonstrated the feasibility of the use of the income tax principle itself and had familiarized the public with the machinery of its administration.   The device was already being extended.   In 1914, when the tax situation in Connecticut was serious and revision became necessary, Professor Seligman suggested to the state legislature and to the tax commissioner of Connecticut the adoption of a state corporate income tax and the utilization of duplicates of the returns made to the federal government.   The suggestion resulted in the adoption of the plan, with the result that a movement for state income taxes based on the federal tax was inaugurated.

The Mayor's Committee reported in January, 1916, and the Mills Committee reported to the legislature in the following month.   In both reports the adoption of a state income tax with a division of the yield between the state and the localities was recommended.   In the report of the Mills Committee the defects of the tax system of the state of New York as it stood at the time the report was made were set forth in an uncompromising fashion:[1]

Were the people of New York once aroused to the full extent of evasions under the present law, another year could not pass without an important tax reform. . . . Our present law is based upon the theory that earning power is fairly represented by property and especially real property.   However, a superficial knowledge of business of today discloses the fact that quite the contrary is true.   As a result of this inconsistency between the law and the fact, we have permitted an important part of our well-to-do citizens

[1] (New York) Joint Legislative Committee on Taxation, *Report*, 1916, p. 28, *et seq.*

to grow up and enjoy large incomes, and therefore large taxpaying ability, without actually requiring them to bear their share of the burden.

In this report the injustices brought about by the operation of the law are pointed out in detail: the burden of the tax upon real estate owners; the " crushing force " of the taxes upon those least able to pay, and the unfairness of the system in its effect upon various classes of persons and enterprises.

The committee answered the question submitted to it by the legislature, namely, " how can the state most equitably and effectively reach all property which should be subjected to taxation and avoid conflict and duplication of taxation on the same property? " in the following concise summary:[1]

. . . All of the evidence presented and all our investigations tend to show that the end sought for will be accomplished best by: (1) the abolition of the present tax on personal property; (2) the withdrawal of general business incomes from the provisions of section 182 of the tax laws; and (3) the imposition of an income tax on individuals and general business corporations, including manufacturing corporations.

The first step was taken with the passage of a corporation income tax law, known as the " Emerson law," in 1917.[2] According to the terms of this law a franchise tax of three per cent was imposed on the net income of manufacturing and mercantile corporations. Two-thirds of the yield of the tax was allotted to the state and one-third to the localities. This law was successful as a revenue-producer, for it yielded $18,000,000 in the first year of its operation, but it was far from being a perfect piece of tax

[1] *Ibid.*, p. 206.
[2] *Laws of New York*, 1917, ch. 726.

legislation.   It was soon found that the larger cities of the
state were not deriving a sufficient amount of revenue from
the new law to make up for the loss of personal taxes, and
protests were soon heard from that quarter.[1]   The nomen-
clature of the act was confusing in its application of the
tax to " manufacturing and mercantile " corporations only.
Moreover, in the light of the additional information about
the operation of state income taxes which was accumula-
ting with each passing year, it became clear that a tax of
this kind, imposed on the net income of corporations, was
only remotely connected with the taxation of personal incomes, and that it was not a tax which could reach the
roots of the trouble with the taxation of intangibles.   Such
a tax as the New York corporation income tax was coming
to be regarded as a *business tax,* closely related to a tax on
real property. This fact was recognized in recommendations
made in 1918 by the committee of the National Tax Association which was appointed to devise a model system of state
and local taxation. In the system recommended by that committee a proportional tax on the net income derived from
business as a tax or excise with respect to carrying on or
doing business is included, but this tax is but one of the
constituent parts of a three-fold system, of which the other
two members are a *personal income tax* and a *property tax.*

Meanwhile other committees were still working on the
question of the personal income tax.   A committee on individuals and partnerships reported at the seventh state conference on taxation in January, 1917, recommending the
adoption of a state income tax.   The Advisory Council of
Real Estate Interests obtained the assistance of Professor
H. A. E. Chandler and proceeded to continue the investi-

[1] Powell, " State Income Tax on Corporations," *Proceedings of the
Eighth State Tax Conference,* 1919, p. 327.

gations begun under Professor Chandler for the Mills Committee. As a result this committee also reported in favor of a personal income tax law. In the annual report for 1918 the state tax commission urgently recommended the adoption of a state income tax law at a low rate and with small deductions. Finally, in 1919, a legislative committee, the " Davenport Committee," was again set to work on the income tax. This committee obtained the services of experts, and made Professor Seligman of Columbia the chairman of one of the sub-committees and Professor Bullock of Harvard the chairman of another. Mr. Laurence A. Tanzer of New York City was counsel for the committee. The various possibilities and alternatives to a personal income tax were thoroughly worked out. Finally a report in favor of a personal income tax was accepted, and early in 1919 the committee presented a bill for the imposition of an income tax. The bill was framed with the greatest possible care and with the advice tnd help of the tax experts whose assistance the committee had enlisted. The bill bore the traces of the same skill and consideration of details which are to be seen in the proposals of the committee on model taxation. It was passed without substantial changes, except for the fact that the administration of the tax was put in the hands of the state comptroller rather than the state tax commission. Thus after years of consideration, the greatest industrial state was enabled to begin the utilization of a personal income tax in the following year, 1920. The adoption of the tax in New York is the result of impartial and far-sighted effort on the part of many interested citizens, but probably most of all to Professor Seligman, who labored indefatigably for the tax from the time of the successful culmination of the efforts for a federal tax to the final passage of the New York income tax law in 1919.

2. *The present income tax law*

According to the personal income tax law passed in New York in 1919 [1] a moderately progressive tax is imposed on the incomes of residents and on the incomes of non-residents from sources within the state. The rates of taxation and the corresponding classes of income are as follows:

Net income	Rate (per cent)
First $10,000	1
Next $40,000	2
Above $50,000	3

In the matter of rates and the degree of progression adopted the New York law failed to follow the federal law or the recommendations of the committee on model taxation. The decision was a wise one with respect to both examples. Such a scale of rates as that used in the imposition of the federal income tax was manifestly absurd if applied to state purposes and taken in conjunction with the decision to include in net income sums paid as income taxes to any jurisdiction. The confiscation of the entire income would be the result in the case of some of the very large incomes the recipients of which are known to be domiciled in New York. Even if such a scale were possible, the result would be so great a revenue to the state that extravagant and wasteful dispositions of the surplus would become the order of the day. The contrast of the scale actually adopted by New York and the scale recommended by the Committee on Model Taxation and illustrated in the draft of a model personal income tax law prepared by that committee is more significant. The progressive scale recommended ranged from one per cent on the first $1,000 of net income to six per cent on net income

[1] *Laws of New York*, 1919, ch. 627.

above $5,000. In view of the careful consideration given
by the framers of the New York law to the point of
view expressed by the committee on model taxation, the
introduction of a more moderate scale in the New York
law illustrates the trend of the times. The high federal
rates must be the background, never to be ignored, of all
income taxes of the present. Only the most moderate
state rates can operate without injustice as long as the
present policy of the federal government is continued. It
is an open question as to whether a simple proportional
rate, as for example, two per cent on net income, might not
be equally satisfactory and accomplish all necessary results,
under the present circumstances. Moreover, the states are
not in need of such great amounts of revenue at the present
time as to necessitate steeply graduated rates.

This tax applies to the incomes of individuals only, as
the incomes of corporations are subject to a separate tax.[1]
Personal exemptions were fixed at $1,000 for the indi-
vidual, $2,000 for the head of a family or for husband and
wife together, and $200 additional for each dependent.[2]
In the definition of gross income and in enumerating the
deductions which are to be made from gross income in the
determination of net income the New York law follows the
federal law fairly closely.

In addition to the specific personal exemptions, interest
on obligations of the United States and its possessions, interest of obligations of the state of New York or of any

----

[1] In 1919 the tax on the net income of corporations was raised from
three to four and one-half per cent and extended to apply to all corporations.

[2] In the law as passed in 1919 these exemptions were denied to non-
residents. The decision of the United States Supreme Court that such
a provision was unconstitutional and the amendment for the New York
law in conformance with this decision are described in subsequent
pages.

municipal corporation or political subdivision thereof; compensation received from the United States; income received by an officer of a religious denomination or by an institution or trust for religious, charitable, philanthropic, educational, or other similar specified purposes and used for such purposes; proceeds of life-insurance policies or annuities; accident or health insurance; and property acquired by gift or bequest were also exempted. Dividends from corporations are included in the income of residents, but excluded from the income of non-residents, except as they form part of the income derived by such non-residents from sources within the state. At the time of the passage of the law this provision was vigorously debated. The dividends received by non-residents could have been taxed only if received from domestic corporations, and it was held that New York institutions would have been unjustly discriminated against if this were done. In order to bring about a fair operation of this principle, not only dividends, but interest on bank deposits, bonds, notes, and sums received as annuities were also exempted in the case of non-residents.

The taxation of dividends received by residents of New York is in itself a departure from the federal law, which allows a partial exemption from the income tax of dividends of corporations. It is becoming increasingly evident that a tax on the net income of corporations is a *business tax,* to be considered as a supplement to the personal income tax rather than as a substitute for it. From this point of view the taxation of the corporate income and the taxation of income received by individuals, even if a part of this latter income is from corporate sources, is no longer regarded as unjust double taxation, unless it operates unequally with respect to different classes of business or different classes of individuals. The real effect of the use of a corporate income tax and an individual income tax in the same jurisdiction is not so much to bring about any unfairness in the tax burden as it is to effect a heavier rate of taxation upon funded incomes than upon unfunded incomes, a policy which is in accordance with the best modern tax theory. Such a policy is particularly adapted to the needs of New York, where the question of a differentiation of the kinds of income and the imposition of a higher rate of tax upon "unearned" incomes was decided in the negative. With regard to differentiation produced in the latter way, it was decided that in the interests of simplicity, and in view of the fact that the graduated rates of the federal tax imposed a heavier burden upon those funded incomes which are in fact found among the larger incomes, no discrimination should be made. The discrimination which is actually produced by the system of taxation now employed is probably slighter than that introduced in the ordinary differentiation plans, less irritating to the taxpayer, and less difficult from the administrative point of view.

The deductions which are permitted in the determination of net income are business expenses, taxes other than income taxes paid to the United States or to any state, losses, worthless debts, interest on indebtedness, and gifts (to the amount of not more than 15 per cent of net income) to religious, charitable, scientific or educational corporations or associations organized under the laws of New York. The law as passed in 1919 contained a provision for the deduction of interest on indebtedness which differed from that contained in the federal law. The state law allowed the deduction of only such a proportion of interest paid as the net taxable income bore to the total income. This provision corresponds to a provision in the preliminary report of the Committee on Model Taxation. That committee called

attention to the fact that the issue by the federal government of large amounts of tax-exempt bonds complicated the
question of the taxation of incomes by the states, and in
suggesting the above plan for limiting interest deducted,
stated its opinion that "any other procedure will tend to
make the personal income tax a farce in many cases and
will give occasion for legitimate complaint." [1] This provision has little to recommend it except its intentions, however, for the calculation is impossible to make, since net income cannot be produced until the amount of deductions
has been determined. It proved unpopular in New York
and the law repealing it was made retroactive to January
1, 1920. [2]

Income taxes were omitted from the list of taxes
deductible from gross income. It was felt that the taxable
base ought not to be affected by the taxes paid to other
jurisdictions. A provision was adopted which was counted
upon to prevent burdensome double taxation in a wholly
different way. A non-resident subject to the income tax of
another state or country is allowed to be credited with such
a proportion of the income tax payable to New York
as his income taxable by New York bears to his entire income taxed by the other state or country, provided the laws
of the latter grant a substantially similar credit to residents
of New York.

At the time of the passage of the personal income tax
law the taxation of intangible personal property as property was abolished, but the taxation of tangible personal
property was allowed to continue.

In matters of administration the New York income tax
law is in most respects in accord with the best modern procedure. The weakness of the older method of local as-

[1] *Preliminary Report*, etc., p. 15.
[2] *Laws of New York*, 1920, ch. 693.

sessment of income taxes had become a matter of universal knowledge by 1919. No other course was open but to provide central administration. The natural disposition of the state income tax was in the hands of the state tax commission, which has charge of the assessment of the franchise tax on corporations. Collection would naturally have gone to the state comptroller. The passage of the income tax law was urged by the state tax commission and opposed by the state comptroller. In the end, and as the result of political considerations, the entire administration of the law, including assessment as well as collection, was left to the state comptroller. The comptroller was empowered to divide the state into income tax districts and to establish branch offices in these districts. In actually working out the system advances were made over the simple directions contained in the law. A state income tax bureau was established as a separate branch of the comptroller's office and Mr. Mark Graves was appointed income tax director, to have entire charge of the administration. It became the practice of the bureau to issue frequent statements, reports, and instructions, and to make the details of the operation of the state income tax matters of common knowledge. In 1921 a new tax commission was organized and the administration of the income tax was put into the hands of the new organization.

With regard to collection and information at the source, New York has undertaken an experiment the outcome of which is still in doubt, although the operation of the law during its first year has been regarded as almost unqualifiedly successful. Collection at the source was adopted for the incomes of non-residents in the law as it was passed in 1919. In order that the employer should not act as judge on a question of residence, it was required that the tax should be deducted in every case in which the salary

amounted to $1,000 or more, unless the employee filed a
certificate that he was a resident of the state. This withholding at the source was required only in the case of
salaries and other compensation for personal services.
Owing to an oversight an unexpected difficulty developed.
The income tax bill in the original form in which it was
presented to the legislature provided for a tax on individual
incomes at a uniform rate of two per cent, and the rate of
withholding stood at two per cent to correspond with the
tax rate. In the course of the discussion of the bill in the
legislature the income tax rates were changed to one, two,
and three per cent on different amounts of income, but the
corresponding change in the amount to be withheld at the
source was neglected. While the first collections were
being made the attorney-general and the comptroller ruled
that an employer need not withhold more than one per
cent on salaries not exceeding $10,000. In May, 1920, the
law was changed so as to provide for withholding for compensation for personal services of non-residents at the rates
of one, two, and three per cent.[1] The provision that residents might be excluded from the withholding by filing
certificates of residence was continued.

The usefulness of such a provision for collection at the
source remains to be demonstrated. At the time when collection at the source was tried under the federal income tax
act dissatisfaction was almost universal. The Committee
on Model Taxation regards collection at the source as undesirable for the reason that the trouble of taxpaying and
possibly even a part of the tax burden itself is passed on
from the person upon whom taxpaying should devolve.
These experimental results concerning collection at the source
are not exactly applicable to New York, however, as the

[1] *Laws of New York*, 1920, ch. 691. Effective May 10, 1920.

withholding in New York applies only to the incomes of non-residents, and only to salaries and the compensation for personal services received by such non-residents. Several other states tax the income of non-residents derived from sources within the state levying the income tax, but aside from New York no state attempts to collect the tax on such incomes at the source. The arguments for collection at the source for incomes of non-residents are good, particularly with respect to the prevention of evasion. It remains to be seen whether the burden imposed upon the persons or corporations paying the compensation for personal services is so heavy that dissatisfaction becomes general.

Information at the source is required very much as under the federal law. Such information is required concerning all payments of $1,000 or more. For failure to make a return, or for fraud, a fine of not more than $1,000 may be imposed and a double tax paid on the tax not originally paid. Lighter penalties are provided for delinquent returns made voluntarily and for delayed tax payments.

Like Wisconsin and Massachusetts, New York distributes a part of the proceeds of the income tax to the localities. At the time when the New York income tax act was passed the needs of the state and the localities for additional revenue were ever-increasing. The income tax promised to satisfy this demand as well as to remedy some of the most conspicuous defects in the existing property tax system. Accordingly the principle of division of yield was adopted. After the retention of a fund of $250,000 for the payment of refunds and abatements, the comptroller was instructed to pay 50 per cent of the remainder into the state treasury and to distribute the equivalent sum among the counties in proportion to the assessed valuations

of real estate in the counties.   The county treasurers were
required to apportion the amount received among the cities
and towns in proportion to the assessed valuations of real
property.   Each city's share goes into the city's general
funds, and each town's share is credited against the amount
of the county tax payable against it.   These provisions bring
about a tendency in the assessment of real estate which
counteracts the ordinary effects of the assessment machinery.   Under the present income tax law, the higher the
assessments in any locality the greater the share of the
proceeeds of the income tax which that locality is entitled
to receive; while the old system encouraged the under-
valuation of real estate so that the localities might lighten
their shares of the general tax.

This requirement of a distribution to the localities of
one-half of the proceeds of the income tax resulted in the
early support for the tax from individuals and localities
which might ordinarily have been sceptical of the effects
upon business of a progressive tax on personal incomes.
In fact, a committee appointed by the Conference of
Mayors came promptly to the assistance of the state comptroller when the constitutionality of the income tax act
was questioned.[1]

The question of the proper distribution of the proceeds
of the income tax is not one which may be answered simply
by pointing to the probable efficacy of the particular plan
adopted in New York in bringing about a better assessment
of real property.   The New York plan has been severely
criticized, principally on the ground that since the income tax is supposed to tap sources of revenue which were
untouched by the general property tax, a distribution according to the assessed value of real estate has little per-

<hr>

[1] *New York Times*, Dec. 14, 1919.

tinence or meaning.[1]   This was acknowledged in a discussion at the annual meeting of the National Tax Association in 1919, when a well-known Wisconsin expert referred to the New York plan as " less logical but more practical " than the Wisconsin plan of distribution according to the derivation of the tax.   The " practical " aspects of the New York plan are apparently conceived to be the appearances of relief with which the local body of taxpayers receive the funds distributed by the state comptroller.   On the other hand, distribution according to source is regarded in Massachusetts as conducive to great injustice, and distribution according to the apportionment of the state tax as a fairer method.[2]   It is plain that income tax method has not yet progressed far enough to yield as definite results with regard to proper distribution as with administration, and the New York plan is neither to be criticized or approved until it has been tried out over a longer period.

The career of the New York provision for the taxation of non-residents was destined to be eventful.   The question of the constitutionality of taxing the incomes of non-residents had been recognized as one which was likely to become pressing since the first application of the Wisconsin law to such incomes.   When this form of taxation was finally determined upon in New York the question took on a new aspect, for New York is unique not only in its tax-paying ability in comparison with the rest of the country but also in the extent to which incomes are earned within its borders by non-residents.   The situation was described by Professor Seligman as follows:[3]

[1] A. E. Holcomb, " State Income Taxes," *Bulletin of the National Tax Association*, vol. vi, no. 4 (Jan. 1921), p. 127.

[2] *Report of the (Massachusetts) Joint Special Committee on Taxation*, 1919, pp. 50, 51.

[3] E. R. A. Seligman, " The Taxation of Non-Residents in the New York Income Tax," *Bulletin of the National Tax Association*, vol. v, no. 2 (Nov. 1919), p. 41.

In many of the less advanced states of the union the great majority of incomes within the state are earned by residents of the state; that is to say, there are comparatively few non-residents who sojourn for a protracted period within the state. And, on the other hand, most of the residents of the state secure all or a very large part of their revenue from property situated or business conducted within the state. In New York, however, the situation is very different. In the first place, New York City, as the great metropolitan center, attracts people from all over the country. Not only do they swarm to New York for weeks or months at a time, but a large number of wealthy individuals, who still retain their legal residence in other states, erect princely mansions in New York and live there most of the year. On the other hand, New York is the financial center of the country: we know that more than one-third of the individual income tax of the entire country is paid in New York. This means that the wealthy residents of New York own a large part of the property of the nation and that the incomes received in New York are to a considerable extent received from sources outside the state. Finally, New York as the industrial center of the country is crowded with hundreds of thousands of members of the professional classes and of wage-earners who get their living in the city but who commute to the suburbs. Northern New Jersey and, to a less extent, southwestern Connecticut, are nothing but suburbs of New York.

Thus from both points of view the question of double taxation, *i. e.*, the taxation of non-residents on income received within the state and of residents on incomes received without the state, assumes in New York a significance which in practice far transcends that in any other part of the country.

In working out the plan which was finally adopted in New York, namely, that of the taxation of non-residents on income derived from sources within the state of New York and the taxation of residents on all income, these facts were carefully taken into consideration. It was plain that the taxation of incomes from within the state only, while practicable in a debtor state like Wisconsin, would mean the exclusion of the high proportion of income received by residents of New York from outside the state. The revenue that New York would receive from its taxpayers would be insignificant compared with the expenditures which it would be called upon to incur because of their presence in the state.   The second possibility, that of allowing exemption from taxation to non-residents, would mean that New Yorkers, working side by side with New Jerseyites, would be subject to taxation and the New Jerseyites would go free.   The third possible solution, that of taxing residents on total income and non-residents on income derived within the state seemed to the framers of the law the least of the three evils.   Injustice to non-residents who were or became subject to personal income taxes was guarded against by a provision suggested by Professor Seligman, by which credit was allowed for income taxes paid in other states provided the other jurisdiction granted similar credits.[1]   It was held that this solution of the problem marked an advance in the development of state income taxes, in line with that of the United States and of other important countries.   The New York law went one step ahead by allowing credit for taxes paid to other jurisdictions.   The sections of the law allowing to *resident* taxpayers personal exemptions of $1,000 and $2,000 was framed on the assumption that neighboring states would soon adopt income tax laws.

Shortly after the passage of the law the fight against it was begun by non-residents.   The litigation was begun by the Yale and Towne Manufacturing Company, a Connecticut corporation doing business in New York, which contended that the provision requiring it to pay to the state of New York a portion of the salaries of its employees who were non-residents of the state of New York was uncon-

[1] E. R. A. Seligman, " The New York Income Tax," *Political Science Quarterly*, vol. xxxiv, no. 4 (Dec. 1919), pp. 536, 537.

stitutional and inconsistent with the " due process of law "
clause of the Fourteenth Amendment. Eventually all
allegations but one were disregarded, and the litigation re-
volved around the question as to whether the New York
law was unconstitutional in depriving non-residents of the
$1,000 and $2,000 exemptions allowed to unmarried and
married residents of New York. The case was eventually
carried to the Supreme Court of the United States. On
March 1, 1920, that court upheld the right of the states
to tax the incomes of non-residents, but held unconstitutional as discriminatory the provision of the New York
law which denied the personal exemptions of $1,000 and
$2,000 to non-residents while granting such exemptions to
residents.[1] Justice Pitney, in delivering the opinion, declared the law discriminatory in the following terms:

In the concrete the particular incident of the discrimination is
upon citizens of Connecticut and New Jersey, neither of which
has an income tax law. Whether they must pay a tax upon the
first $1,000 to $2,000 of income, while their [New York] asso-
ciates do not, makes a substantial difference. We are unable to
find ground for the discrimination, and are constrained to hold
that it is an unwarranted denial to the citizens of Connecticut
and New Jersey of the privileges and immunities enjoyed by the
citizens of New York.

The suggestion made by the counsel for New York that
the states affected might make counter discriminations
against residents of New York was dismissed with the de-
claration that " discrimination cannot be cured by retalia-
tion."

The adverse decision was anticipated by the New York
officials, and an amendment was at once introduced in the
legislature granting non-residents the same exemptions as

[1] Eugene M. Travis, Comptroller, *v.* The Yale & Towne Mfg. Co., U.
S. Supreme Court, March 1, 1920.

those previously granted to residents.[1] In the same legislative session the deductions allowed to non-residents were
made to correspond with those allowed to residents.[2] The
New York law is now safeguarded from further attacks
along this line, but the taxation of non-residents is still a
source of active dissatisfaction in the "commuting" class.

3. *The revenue from the tax*

The proceeds of the tax on personal incomes were
counted upon to make good the deficit in the state's
revenues which would otherwise have resulted from
the enforcement of prohibition, and at the same time
to supplement the revenues of the state and the localities
from other sources. The tax has fulfilled the expectations
of its proponents in this respect. The rates as finally
adopted, reaching a maximum of three per cent on amounts
above $50,000, were expected to produce a tax yield of
$45,000,000.[3] The yield of the tax for the first year,
approximately $37,000,000, was below the most optimisic
of the estimates made at the time of the passage of the act,
but it exceeded by many millions any sum ever produced
by the personal income tax in any other state, and was regarded as a satisfactory yield by the state officials. More
than $22,000,000 was received from New York City alone.
In all, nearly 600,000 residents of the state paid taxes on
their incomes, and more than 25,000 non-residents paid income taxes.

In accordance with the legal requirement, one-half of
the proceeds of the income tax were distributed to the various counties of the state. More than $18.250,000 was

[1] *Laws of New York*, 1920, ch. 191.

[2] *Laws of New York*, 1920, ch. 693.

[3] *Bulletin of the National Tax Association*, vol. v, no. 8 (May, 1919),
p. 204.

distributed in this way, according to the valuation of real property. New York City's share was $12,469,255. In this instance New York City profited by its 100 per cent valuation of real property, and the taxpayers who were accustomed to protest against their heavy assessments were to some extent recompensed by the receipts from the new source of revenue.

An analysis of the federal income tax returns for New York shows that the receipts from the New York state income tax for the year 1919 were about 10 per cent of the personal income taxes collected by the federal government in New York in the preceding year.[1] New York is by far the richest state in the union, and is counted upon by the federal government to furnish about one-third of the total yield of the country's personal income tax. The net incomes upon which the taxes are paid in New York formed only about one-sixth of the total net incomes for the whole country, however. A comparison of these two ratios indicates that a number of very large incomes must be received in New York state, and that the very high graduated rates of the federal scheme produce a disproportionately high tax yield when applied to these extremely large incomes. An income tax with low rates and a slight degree of progression, like the state income tax, is not expected to produce such amounts. The state tax, which is applied at the uniform rate of three per cent to all amounts of income above $50,000, hardly taps the funds reached by the high federal tax. New York ranks behind Wisconsin and Massachusetts in the ratio of state income tax receipts to federal income tax receipts, but an attempt to gain larger amounts from the New York state tax is regarded by tax experts as inadvisable on almost every count. New

[1] United States Internal Revenue, *Statistics of Income for 1918*, p. 24.

York had 40 resident individuals with incomes of
$1,000,000 and over in 1918,[1] subject to a federal tax of
73 per cent on that part of the income in excess of
$1,000,000; such incomes, and even those of smaller
amounts, could hardly bear a heavy state tax without confiscation, an effect which is not contemplated or desired
under the present system.

The New York income tax has already come to play an
important part in the state revenue. The total revenue
receipts of the state for the year ending June 30, 1920 were
$115,591,607,[2] of which sum the income tax payments
made into the state treasury were $16,500,000, or approxi-
mately one-seventh. If the entire proceeds of the income
tax had been assigned to the state about one-fourth of the
state revenues would have come from taxes on personal
incomes. The income tax proved to be unexpectedly productive, and at the close of the fiscal year the income tax
bureau held undistributed the sum of $1,700,000. An un-
fortunate tendency has developed to regard the state's share
of the income tax as a surplus, for the proceeds are not assigned to any particular purpose.

The cost of administration of the New York tax for the
first year was approximately $1,000,000, or between two
and three per cent of the amount collected. The cost of
organizing and installing an administrative bureau must of
course be unusually large during the first year, and this
figure may be expected to show an appreciable decrease.
During 1920 the income tax office handled 826,000 returns,
so that the cost of collection as related to the number of
returns was a little more than a dollar for each return.
The work of an income tax office is divided into two parts.

[1] United States Internal Revenue, *Statistics of Income for 1918*, p. 67.
[2] New York Comptroller, *Report*, 1920, p. xiii.

During the first part of the year the office handles the voluntary payments, and during the remaining months delinquent payments and understatements are cared for. Viewed in this way, the New York income tax bureau may be said to have collected $36,250,000 in voluntary payments at a cost to the state of only $250,000, and to have sustained itself, approximately, during the rest of the year.[1] The voluntary collections were made at a cost of less than one per cent.

4. *Unsettled questions*

The adoption of a personal income tax law by the state of New York is an event hardly to be overstimated in the history of state income taxes. The experiment begun in Wisconsin eight years before, significant as it was, could not settle the question of the suitability of the income tax to a highly organized industrial and commercial area, for Wisconsin stands far down on the list of manufacturing states. The experience of Massachusetts was more significant in pointing out the way in which the income tax can be adapted to an increasingly complex economic organization, but the Massachusetts tax was not a general income tax, and, in the second place, Massachusetts, rich as it is, holds only one-third of the taxable income contained in New York. When New York itself, the richest state in the union on almost all counts, and the source of a third of the federal income taxes, succeeds in installing a workable income tax system and in obtaining a sum equivalent to more than one-fourth of the state revenues from taxes on personal incomes, the revenue-yielding capacity of income taxes can no longer be called into question. Improvements in the plan of taxation itself and in the administrative

---

[1] Information furnished by New York Income Tax Director Jan. 14, 1921.

machinery involved will undoubtedly be made; the tax itself may give way to other forms of taxes as revenue needs change and the social structure is modified; but the one almost universal count against the personal income tax as affairs stood in 1911, that of a failure to produce revenue, has ceased to exist. Curiously enough, one of the income tax problems which seems likely to be serious is its *over-productiveness,* and the consequent temptation to extravagance which surplus revenues always produce.

The dimensions of the income tax system in New York intensify the problems which have arisen in connection with other state income taxes but which have sometimes been overlooked. The New York plan of tax rates, for example, (that of a graduated tax which reaches a maximum at three per cent on taxable incomes of more than $50,000) remains to be tested. During the first year of its operation, when the federal tax rates reached a maximum of 73 per cent, it appeared to be well suited to the whole tax situation. If the projected reduction of the federal surtax rates is brought about, should the New York tax rates be raised? Or should they be *lowered* for the same reasons which are urged for the reduction of the federal rates, and such a flat rate as that of the two per cent originally planned for New York be substituted? The productiveness of the tax in a few given years is not the only factor to be considered; the effect of the tax payments upon the status of large incomes and the domiciles of their recipients, together with many less definable social effects, must also be taken into account. Should a distinction be made between earned and unearned income for the purposes of taxation? Unearned or " investment " incomes are probably received in larger amounts in New York than in any other state. One of the early advocates of the New York tax believes that such a distinction should have been made, at least for the lower stages of income, since the heavier rates which in practice apply principally to incomes derived in considerable part from property do not affect these incomes.[1] Should the exemption of intangible property have been accompanied by the exemption of tangible property? The same authority holds that the present practice of exempting tangible property should have been made a legal practice.

The questions involved in the taxation of non-residents are only partially settled. Now that non-residents of New York are allowed exemptions similar to those of residents, the right of the state to apply the tax in its present form to the income of non-residents appears to be established. The United States Supreme Court decision in the case of the taxation of non-residents by Oklahoma[2] established the dominion of the states over the persons, property and business within their borders, the right of the states to levy taxes upon the incomes of non-residents from property or business within the state, and the right of the states to enforce the payment of such taxes by the exercise of their control over the property within their borders. This right of taxation has been constructed to apply to the income of non-resident exporters whose business offices are in the state of New York, on the ground that the tax is upon net income derived from conducting business in New York and not upon business itself.[3] The fact that such taxpayers' homes are outside New York bears directly upon the question of enforcing tax payment, but not upon the right of the state to assess the income tax in such cases.

Thus far, then, the state's *right* to tax the incomes of

[1] Seligman, *op. cit.*, p. 542.

[2] Charles B. Shaffer *v.* Frank C. Carter, State Auditor, and Abner Bruce, Sheriff of Creek County, Oklahoma, U. S. Supreme Court, March 1, 1920.

[3] *New York Times*, March 12, 1921.

non-residents, if no discrimination is involved, is clear as
matters stand at present. The *wisdom* of making the attempt is more questionable. Mr. Holcomb, secretary of
the National Tax Association, concludes a review of the
Oklahoma and New York decisions with the following
words:[1]

The reviewer looks with no little concern upon the whole problem
of non-resident income taxation, not only because of its doubtful
expediency, but more because of his inability to see how a fair,
thorough and effective system of collection is to be obtained. The
difficulties of enforcing tax warrants for personal taxes against
non-residents have long been recognized by the New York courts.
. . . If we are to have a repetition of the farce with respect to
non-resident income taxes which has obtained with respect to
property taxes, it would appear altogether better to resort to
some other form of business taxes. . . .

The Committee on Model Taxation also advocates the
taxation of residents only, on the ground that the income
tax is properly a tax upon persons only, to be collected at
places where they are domiciled, and not upon business;
and that a well-constructed system of taxation involves
taxing business and property located within a state by
other means, so that such business and property can in no
wise be regarded as escaping taxation. Professor Bullock,
the chairman of the Committee on Model Taxation, stated
that " from the theoretical point of view the New York
law as it stands, is bad, except for this saving clause by
which it recognizes the right of other states to step in and
levy personal income taxes without doubly taxing." In
spite of the opposition on theoretical grounds, the taxation
of non-residents still has warm support from within the

[1] *Bulletin of the National Tax Association,* vol. v, no. 6 (March,
1920), p. 183.

[2] *Proceedings of the National Tax Association,* 1919, p. 406.

state, and the final solution of the problem waits for further evidence.

Still another question which is yet to be worked out in New York is that of collection at the source of taxes on the incomes of non-residents. The main argument for the use of the method is the incontrovertible one that it is the only really effective means of obtaining taxes due from persons resident outside of the state.   In the Yale and Towne case, whch had its origin in the refusal of a withholding agent to withhold the percentage of payments made to its employees which the New York income tax law specified, it was held that the right of the state to impose a tax upon the incomes of non-residents arising from business or occupations carried on within its borders carried with it the right to enforce payment " so far as it can by the exercise of a just control over persons and property within the state, as by garnishment of credits (of which the withholding provision of the New York law is the practical equivalent)." [1]   It was held that in the case of non-residents the state merely adopted a convenient substitute for the personal liability which it could not impose.   It was also held that the burden imposed upon the withholding agent was not an unjust one and not an unreasonable regulation of the conduct of business within the state.

The question of collection at the source is linked up with the taxation of non-residents so closely that if the latter goes the former goes with it.   The experience of the state of New York ought to furnish a conclusive demonstration of the practicability of the method.   Meanwhile many critics remain as sceptical of the ultimate success of the means as of the permanent value of the non-resident taxation itself.

[1] *Bulletin of the National Tax Association*, vol. v, no. 6 (March, 1920), p. 183.

In the collection of a tax of the dimensions of the New York income tax, questions which are in the last analysis questions of the accounting methods sanctioned by the state loom up in great importance. In March, 1921, such a question presented itself, at the very time when income tax computations were being made. The question arose in connection with the assessment of federal income taxes. When Solicitor General Frierson announced that excess realized on the sale of stocks was no longer to be considered as constituting taxable income under the federal law, —a decision which was announced to the United States Supreme Court in connection with the case of *Goodrich* vs. *Edwards*,—taxpayers under the New York income tax law were thrown into confusion. The New York income tax bureau, which had followed the policy of levying against payers of the income tax on any excess realized on the sale of stocks and bonds, at once announced that it would continue its former policy, and would not interpret section 353 of the state law in the way in which the federal law was to be interpreted according to the new decision. The difficulty which was immediately emphasized by the opponents of the state's policy was the fact that when a tax is levied on the excess realized from the sale of stocks above the market value on January 1, 1919, when the state income tax law became effective, the taxpayer may have incurred an actual loss in the transaction, on account of the price paid in purchase before January 1, 1919. At the time the above decision was announced the case of the People ex rel. Edward Klauber, a New York lace manufacturer, against Comptroller James A. Wendell, was being heard in the Appellate Division at Albany. The case was similar to that of the Goodrich case in the United State Supreme Court, and the position taken by the counsel for Mr. Klauber was that the state must confine its tax to income and that it lacks the power to turn a loss into a theoretical profit. The decision was expected in May, 1921, and the case was to be taken before the Court of Appeals in the following month.

After the federal decision the state policy was attacked with increasing vigor, and the director of the income tax bureau announced that he had laid the matter before the senate and assembly tax committees with the suggestion that a change in the state income tax law should be considered. The provision had been condemned as " unduly harsh " by the committee on model taxation, with whom the director had conferred. The model tax committee suggested the use of a rule by which the taxpayer is given the benefit of the higher of two estimates at the date of the tax,—basis cost or market value. In the meantime, the director reminded the taxpayers, the income tax bureau had no choice but to administer the law is it stood.

Later in the same month the United States Supreme Court announced a decision establishing the rule that unless a given transaction which was completed prior to the basic date for computation prescribed in the federal law resulted in an actual gain, no " income " could result. It then became a more urgent question as to whether the state of New York could continue to maintain its stand with regard to January, 1919, values, for although the state is not hedged about by the same constitutional limitations, the aim and methods of the laws should be as consistent as possible.

In May, 1921, two events occurred which tended to clear up the matter. The Third Appellate Division handed down decisions denying the right of the state to tax stocks sold at a loss, and a bill was signed which changed the method of computing profit and loss, with the intention of doing away with the injustice which the older method had produced. It was expected that the construction of the state law in the cases not covered by the ruling of the court would still present troublesome complications. The situation illustrates the difficulties of the administration of the income tax in highly developed financial communities.

The distribution of the proceeds of the income tax to the local units is not yet universally approved, and the particular scheme of distribution adopted by New York, that of dividing the proceeds of the income tax among the counties according to assessed valuation, has few supporters. Distribution according to educational needs seems to be coming ino favor, and if New York is not to lag behind the rest of the country in this matter it should give further consideration to the possibilities of such a plan. The possible over-productiveness of the income tax in New York has already been referrel to. Coupled with the program of economy undertaken early in 1921, the great productiveness of the tax may bring about unforeseen problems if a more careful plan of distribution is not made.

Finally, New York has not yet come to know its own mind with respect to the administration of the income tax. When the law was passed in 1919 the usual functions of the state tax commission were disregarded, and the work given to the state comptroller, although the state tax commission continued to administer the corporation taxes. In the following two years an extensive organization was built up and large sums collected with a fair degree of economy. Suddenly, in 1921, the state tax commission was organized and awarded the tax-collecting powers of the comptroller and the secretary of state. The type of organization of tax functions is in accord with the best modern opinion and with the recommendations of the committee on model taxation, but it is probable that the state will encounter temporary difficulties in making the change.

It was not to be expected, even with the wealth of expert assistance which was at hand while the New York income tax law was being worked out, that a perfect system could be evolved in the first year. It is in fact remarkable that a fiscal device which was in general disrepute as a state measure less than ten years before could have been made a uniquely productive source of revenue, and that it could have been employed without active opposition and other undesirable social and political consequences. The questions which remain in part unsettled,—the rates of the tax in relation to the federal rates, the various aspects of the taxation of non-residents and the collection of those taxes, the distribution of the yield, the best type of general and local administration of the tax as it is used in New York, and other more evanescent questions of the proper computation of the taxes,—are in fact, important as they are in bringing about justice and fairness in taxation, matters which are minor in importance when the great fact of the acceptance of the income tax by the public is given its proper place. If an increasingly skillful use is made of this means of taxation, New York will be enabled to occupy a place of as great significance in the field of tax laws and administration as it already does in the field of business finance.

CHAPTER VIII

THE NORTH DAKOTA INCOME TAX

1. *The income tax law of 1919*

NORTH DAKOTA, one of the newer states, made few significant contributions to taxation history until recently. In 1919, however, largely as a result of the influence of the Non-Partisan League in the state, the legislature carried through an extensive program of changes in the tax and revenue code which included the inauguration of an income tax along unusual lines. At the same time provision was made for several state industrial undertakngs. The impelling motive for the adoption of an income tax law seemed to be not so much the usual accumulation of dissatisfaction with the operation of the personal property tax along particular lines as a conviction among the legislators that the existing scheme of taxation exacted contributions for the support of the state from the wrong people,—those not best able to contribute. As a result the effort was made to obtain more revenue from the richest individuals and those who were the recipients of " unearned " income.

The income tax law passed in 1919,[1] therefore, made a distinction between "earned " and " unearned " income and imposed a doubly heavy progressive rate on unearned income up to $12,000 at which point the two sets of rates begin to converge. The law applied the tax to the income of both residents and non-residents,[2] from all sources within

[1] *Laws of North Dakota,* 1919, ch. 23.

[2] Income of non-residents from personal services and intangibles was exempt.

the state. The personal exemptions were $1,000 for the individual, $2,000 for the head of a family, and $200 additional for each dependent person above the number of one. Deductions for ordinary business expenses, losses, bad debts, depreciation, interest on indebtedness, and taxes were allowed. Personal property tax receipts were allowed as offsets. Collection at the source of interest, dividends, profits, premiums, and annuities was provided for, but this provision was later repealed. The proceeds were to defray the general expenses of the state government.

The type of administration provided for was along the lines which have proved most successful in recent years. The tax commissioner was given the supervision of the system and was authorized to divide the state into income tax districts and to appoint special assessors of income, although he might " appoint an existing tax officer to act as such income tax assessor."

The scale of taxation of incomes was as follows:

| *Net income* | *Rate (per cent)* | |
	Earned income	*Unearned income*
1st $1,000	.25	.5
2nd 1,000	.5	1.
3rd 1,000	.75	1.5
4th 1,000	1.	2.
5th 1,000	1.25	2.5
6th 1,000	1.5	3.
7th 1,000	1.75	3.5
8th 1,000	2.	4.
9th 1,000	2.25	4.5
10th 1,000	2.5	5.
11th 1,000	2.75	6.
12th 1,000	3.	6.
13th 1,000	3.25	6.
14th 1,000	3.5	6.
15th 1,000	3.75	6.
16th 1,000	4.	6.

17th	1,000	4.25	6.
18th	1,000	4.5	6.
19th	1,000	4.75	6.
20th	1,000	5.	6.
In excess of $20,000 and not in excess of $30,000		6.	8.
In excess of $30,000 and not in excess of $40,000		8.	10.
In excess of $40,000		10.	10.

A corporation income tax imposed under the same law was levied at the rate of three per cent on net income, plus five per cent of any amount undistributed six months after the end of the fiscal year.

2. *Criticisms of the law of 1919*

Critical comment on the act of 1919 has been general. Not only was the discrimination between earned and un-earned incomes by means of a graduated tax with doubled rates on the unearned income an innovation in this country, but the maximum rates of taxation (10 per cent) were un-precedented in state income taxation. Such a plan of tax-ation has been usually regarded as more suitable for a highly developed community, with large incomes and vested in-terests of long standing, than for a community in which industrial and commercial affairs are in an almost pioneer stage. The whole body of legislation enacted in the ses-sion of 1919 was apparently the work of a body of legisla-tors determined to place so-called " capitalistic " activities at a disadvantage, and significantly, appears as *The New Day in North Dakota: Some of the Principal Laws enacted by the Sixteenth Legislative Assembly, 1919,* the compila-tion of laws of that year published by the state industrial commission. Much of the fiscal legislation bears the mark of this intention rather than of the results of a careful analysis of the financial situation of North Dakota.

Collection at the source involves many problems which have already hampered the authorities.[1]

This system of collection must involve tremendous administrative difficulties and complications, for the withholding agents are required to deduct from each payment of interest, dividends, or other form of taxable income, such part as will be required to pay the tax, and there are no less than twenty-three different rates any one of which may be the proper one in a given case.

Furthermore, double taxation, produced in this case by requiring the taxation of dividends as unearned income but permitting no deductions to the individual for taxes paid by corporations subject to the act frequently has undesirable results.

The defects in the act of 1919 which became apparent almost immediately had to do with the scale of rates and the differentiation between earned and unearned incomes. The income tax was apparently constructed with the intention of promoting social justice through the medium of compulsory contributions to the expenses of the state. The incomes of the wealthy were to be drawn upon for large amounts, in a proportion almost unparalleled in the history of the state taxation of incomes, while only nominal sums were to be exacted from the persons in receipt of small incomes. When the primary rates of the North Dakota act (one-fourth of one per cent on the first $1,000 of taxable earned income and one-half of one per cent on the corresponding category of unearned income) were devised, several signs of the times were already pointing out a safe course for state income taxes which should probably have been heeded in North Dakota. The committee on a model system of state and local taxation appointed by the National

[1] H. L. Lutz, " The Progress of State Taxation since 1911," *American Economic Review*, vol. x, no. 1 (March, 1920), p. 73.

Tax Association had already reported against a smaller initial rate than one per cent. The expense of collecting small tax bills due from persons with low incomes had already received attention in states where the income tax seemed a doubtful success, and changes were imminent. Furthermore, for the first time the actual status of individuals with respect to their incomes was becoming a matter of common knowledge, through the operation of the federal income tax and the publication of *Statistics of Income* by the United States Internal Revenue. A cursory examination of the published figures would have shown that the tax-paying capacity of North Dakota incomes was exceedingly small, both absolutely and relatively, and that such a tax as that provided for in 1919 might be expected to yield only a small amount and to be expensive to administer.

The federal income taxes received in 1917 from North Dakota incomes in 1916 amounted to only five-hundredths of one per cent of the personal income taxes collected in the country as a whole.[1] The tax itself amounted to $66,344, and the number of individuals making returns was 1,176. The federal tax for the year 1916 applied to incomen of $3,000 and over ($4,000 in the case of married persons) and was imposed at the normal rate of two per cent, with surtaxes reaching 13 per cent on the largest incomes. It should have been clear that little return was to be expected from the state tax on large incomes. For the incomes of the year 1917, when the federal tax reached down to incomes of $1,000, the number of returns from North Dakota increased by nearly 20,000. But earned incomes of $4,000 and less were taxed at less than one per cent in North Dakota. The majority, presumably, were

[1] United States Internal Revenue, *Statistics of Income for 1917*, pp. 8, 11.

taxed at one-fourth of one per cent, as the number in receipt of incomes of $1,000 but less than $2,000 has always
proved to be larger than that contained in any other classification of similar size.   The yield of the North Dakota
tax was plainly destined to be small, as the large incomes
were too scarce to produce much revenue and the small in-
incomes were inadequately taxed.

A difficult aspect of the differentiation soon presented
itself.   The tax on unearned incomes failed to prove a
productive source of revenue, not only because the large
incomes were so few in number, but because the rates were
so fixed that in many instances the tax yield of incomes was
smaller than if a simple scale applicable to all incomes alike
had been in force.   The state tax department early recognized the difficulty, and made plans for recommending a
change at the earliest possible time.   The department describes the situation as follows: [1]

Our experience with the earned and unearned feature of the law
has shown us that, in this state at least, such classification is without value. . . . The purpose of taxing the unearned income at a
higher rate is to make such classes of income bear a larger proportion of the burden of income taxation.   Our law has not accomplished this result for the reason that we find in this state practically all individuals have as much, if not more, earned income
than unearned income.   Therefore, since our rates start at the
primary rates in both instances, our present law results in less
revenue than if we taxed the entire income of all individuals at
the earned rate.

An example of the working of the law of 1919 in this respect is furnished by the return of an individual taxpayer
with $20,000 earned income and $1,000 unearned income.
Under the provisions of the law, the rate on the twentieth
thousand of earned incomes is 5 per cent.   The rate on the

---

[1] North Dakota Tax Department, *Statement,* July, 1920.

thousand of unearned income (classified as the first thousand of unearned income) is one-half of one per cent. But if the same individual had an income of $21,000 all earned, the rate on the additional thousand (the twenty-first thousand of earned income) would be six per cent. Consequently the state loses, by this classification, the difference between a tax of six per cent on the additional thousand and a tax of one-half of one per cent on that amount.

The individual who pays taxes on earned income is discriminated against in another way, in respect to increases in the rate of his tax. One critic described the situation as follows:[1]

The rates applying to the two classes of income are elaborately and, in the writer's judgment, uselessly graduated. . . . The rates rise steadily for both classes of income, and the total tax burden on given amounts of the two classes of income presents the singular phenomenon of a heavier rate of increase on the earned incomes than on the unearned. . . . The increases of taxes for the third $10,000 of earned income over the second $10,000 is 54.8 per cent, while for the same amount of unearned income it is . . . 33⅓ per cent. This discrepancy was hardly intended and was produced by introducing, after $10,000, much larger income brackets for unearned income, while the minute graduation of rate for earned income was continued through $20,000 of income.

3. *The operation of the income tax law*

The amount of the income tax certified to the North Dakota state treasurer for collection up to October 1, 1920, was $53,887. During the same year the operation of the corporation income tax, which yielded approximately $460,000, was regarded as satisfactory. The explanation of the small amount of income assessed against individuals

---

[1] Lutz, *op. cit.*, p. 73.

is given as follows in the report of the state tax commissioner: [1]

1. Income from mortgages secured on North Dakota property and income from North Dakota bank deposits were exempt.
2. Dividends received in 1919 earned in 1918 were exempt.
3. Crop failures in 1919 reduced the incomes of both farmers and business men.
4. There are few large incomes in North Dakota, and the personal property tax offset operated to reduce the yield from that part of the tax.
5. The rates on individual incomes are " absurdly low."
6. A large proportion of the individuals with large incomes claimed deductions for taxes paid on national bank stock.
7. The classification of earned and unearned income has involved a loss of revenue.

The tax commissioner's comment on the failure of the present income tax system is as follows: [2]

The personal income tax law has proven a failure as a revenue producer. The larger part of the cost of administration of our income tax law is chargeable to the administration of the personal income tax. More than eighteen thousand personal income tax reports were received from individuals, and over four thousand were received from corporations. The larger part of the corporations were taxable. A large majority of individuals making an income tax report paid only a very small tax or were exempt. It is very probable that if all of the reporting taxpayers had been thoroughly conversant with our income tax law and with the various exemptions and deductions allowable under said law, that we could not have secured nearly as large an amount of revenue as was secured. . . .

[1] North Dakota Tax Commissioner, *Report,* 1919 and 1920, pp. 38, 39.
[2] *Ibid.,* pp. 39, 40, 41.

. . . Sentiment in the state is almost unanimously in favor of an income tax law. There are certain features in our income tax law, however, which are generally considered objectionable. The law is complicated, and consequently the blanks are necessarily complicated and difficult for taxpayers to properly fill out. There is considerable objection to the discrimination shown in our present law in the taxation of small corporations in comparison with the taxation of competing businesses of individuals and partnerships. Corporations pay a tax of three per cent on their net income and no deduction is allowed for personal property taxes paid to the state or local government. The stockholders of the corporation pay a personal income tax on dividends received from the corporation. Dividends are considered unearned income and are subject to the rates provided for unearned income. A business conducted by an individual or partnership is not subject to the income tax. The individual owner or partner pays a tax on his share of the profits of the business, his profits being considered earned income, and consequently taxable at one-half the rate of unearned income. In addition to this, the individual owner or partner, in the case of a partnership, is allowed to deduct his personal property tax in this state, from the amount of his income tax. The result is that the individual owner of an ordinary business pays no tax on the earnings of the business and pays no individual income tax on account of the personal property tax offset.

Further evidence of the comparative failure of the state personal income tax in its present form is given in the fact that the receipts bear the approximate ratio of one to one hundred to the total state tax. They form slightly more than two per cent of the amount collected in North Dakota in 1918 incomes by the federal agents.

The cost of administration of the personal and corporation income taxes combined is stated by the tax commissioner to be 1.65 per cent of the collections.[1] The commissioner notes the fact, however, that the larger part of the cost of administration is chargeable to the personal income

[1] North Dakota Tax Commissioner, *Report,* 1919 and 1920, p. 39.

tax. More than 18,000 individual returns were handled, while only slightly more than 4,000 corporation reports were received. Furthermore, the cost of clerical assistance charged against the income tax does not include an amount representing the use of a considerable part of the office force of the tax commissioner's office for three months.

The following table shows the income tax of individuals classified according to the amount of tax assessed:[1]

Amount of tax assessed	Number assessed	Amount of tax	Per cent of total tax	Average tax per taxpayer
Total, all groups	6,431	$53,887.17	100.00	$8.49
Under $50	6,152	26,899.42	49.90	4.37
$50 and less than $100	104	6,950.83	12.90	66.83
$100 and less than $200	57	7,895.04	14.65	138.51
$200 and less than $500	22	6,246.04	11.59	283.91
$500 and less than $1,000	4	2,615.11	4.85	653.78
Over $1,000	2	3,280.73	6.09	1,640.36

The table given above illustrates the difficulties and expense of collecting the personal income tax in North Dakota under the system put in force in 1919. With 97 per cent of the taxpayers classified paying a total tax of less than $50, a tax which in fact averaged $4.37, the expenses of collection must have been proportionately very large for the small incomes. If it were feasible to calculate the expense of collecting taxes on the lower classifications of incomes, startling results might be obtained, results which might influence the construction of laws in the future, or might at least make clear the fact that the justification of such taxes lies in the moral effect on the taxpayer rather than in the resulting additions to the state revenue.

4. *The future of the income tax in North Dakota*

The urgent recommendations made to the legislature of 1921 by the state tax commissioner were principally con-

[1] North Dakota Tax Commissioner, *Report,* 1919 and 1920, p. 40.

cerned with the extension of the tax to various exempted classes of income, increases in the rates, and a change in the differentiation plan.

A scale of taxation on personal incomes starting at one per cent on the first $1,000 of taxable income was recommended. This tax was to reach six per cent at amounts in excess of $10,000. The suggested scale was modeled on the Wisconsin income tax rates for individuals, but it advanced slightly more rapidly, and reached its maximum at a point $2,000 below that at which the Wisconsin rate becomes six per cent. The recommended rates should be put in force, in the opinion of the tax commissioner, only if his recommendation for the repeal of the personal property tax was also followed. In that case, the income tax should be apportioned to the counties and local districts. If the repeal of the personal property tax laws of the state should not be carried through, at least farm machinery, tools, wearing apparel, and household furniture should be exempted.

The reasons given for the recommended substitution of the income tax for the personal property tax are these:[1]

1. Net income is a more accurate measure of ability to pay than the amount of personal property owned.
2. Persons with incomes can be equitably assessed through the income tax, while all persons who own personal property can not be equitably assessed under the personal property tax.

With regard to the revision of the income tax law of North Dakota, the tax commissioner further recommended to the legislature of 1921 that differentiation (that is, the application of different rates to earned and unearned income) should be abolished. Instead, a graduated surtax should be imposed on unearned incomes, in addition to the normal

[1] North Dakota Tax Commissioner, *Report,* 1919 and 1920, p. 41.

tax. In this way one of the fiscal anomalies of the 1919 law (the situation in which the state receives a smaller revenue from certain combinations oĭ earned and unearned income than from incomes wholly earned) would be done away with.

Other recommendations for the improvement of the personal income tax system were as follows:

The repeal of the personal property tax credit.

The inclusion of income from mortgages secured on business transacted in North Dakota.

The inclusion of income from mortgages secured on North Dakota real property and income from North Dakota bank deposits. In this connection the principle repeatedly enunciated by the National Tax Association's committee on a model system of taxation is presented: " Every person domiciled in the state should make a direct personal contribution toward the support of the state if such person has any taxable ability."

The maintenance of the existing exemptions, largely because of the trouble and expense of levying income taxes on small incomes.

The extension of the three per cent tax imposed on the incomes of corporations to all business carried on within the state under whatever form conducted. Otherwise, dividends received from a corporation already taxed on its net income should be exempted from taxation. The double taxation involved in the taxation of dividends becomes objectionable only when all taxpayers are not given the same treatment.

The inclusion in the permitted deductions of all losses actually sustained during the year in transactions entered into for profit.

Since the above recommendations were made the entire

financial program of North Dakota has met serious opposition and the future of the Non-Partisan League's proposals has become very problematical. It is possible that the income tax, since it is not a form of taxation peculiar to North Dakota, may escape in any general upheaval which occurs. At the time of writing, however,[1] such questions as those of its particular form have been almost lost sight of. The legislature of 1921 failed to pass any constructive tax legislation. In spite of the fact that the personal income tax in North Dakota is a part of a program the whole course of which is doubtful, and has been handicapped by the unusually serious difficulties which its form brought upon it in the first year of its operation, the tax can still be so changed and adapted that it will form a valuable part of the state revenue system. Through the failures of the first year the tax-yielding capacity of the various classes of income has been shown up very clearly. If more extensive use were made of the federal statistics of income, in the way in which those figures have been used by the special revenue commission of New Mexico, for example, the tax-paying power of the state at various hypothetical income tax rates and the yield of any proposed measure might be foretold with a fair degree of accuracy. A number of well-informed agencies and individuals are already urging careful and constructive changes in the law. The chief danger seems to be that North Dakota will fail to recognize the very obvious fact that the state is an agricultural state, with few large fortunes and few unearned incomes, even though the tax commissioner's report presents statistical proof that such is the case. If the state's needs are carefully studied the future income tax can be far more effective than the tax of the first year.

[1] Early in 1921.

CHAPTER IX

THE INCOME TAX MOVEMENT IN NEW MEXICO AND ALABAMA

1. *The New Mexico income tax*

THE state of New Mexico, admitted to the union in 1910, made its first experiment with the taxation of incomes in 1919. In that year the legislature passed an income tax law imposing a graduated tax on the net income of resident individuals and domestic partnerships and corporations and on the income from mines, oil wells and gas wells arising from sources within the state.[1] Deductions were permitted for interest on indebtedness, repairs and insurance, taxes, business expenses, losses, bad debts, and income from partnerships and corporations already taxed under the act. The personal exemptions were $1,000 for each single head of a family, $2,000 for each married head of a family, and $200 for each dependent. The rates of taxation were as follows:

Net income					Rate (per cent)
Above $5,000 and not exceeding $10,000					½ of 1
" 10,000	"	"	"	15,000	¾ of 1
" 15,000	"	"	"	20,000	1
" 20,000	"	"	"	30,000	1½
" 30,000	"	"	"	40,000	2
" 40,000	"	"	"	50,000	2½
" 50,000					3

Personal property tax receipts were to be accepted as off-

[1] *Laws of New Mexico*, 1919, ch. 123.

sets against income taxes. The state treasurer was to administer the act, but no special authorization was given for the appointment of income tax deputies or the defining of income tax districts. The taxes paid were assigned to the state treasury for use in connection with the educational and other state institutions.

The bill was apparently drawn hastily, and questions as to its constitutionality were soon brought up. As a result the governor's call to a special legislative session in February, 1920, including among the subjects for consideration an amendment of the income tax law " in such manner as to make the law non-discriminative, and otherwise to make it conformable to the constitutional limitations on that subject, or else to take such other legislative action in regard thereto as to the legislature may appear to be right and proper." [1]

A new income tax bill, substituting a more elaborate income tax, was introduced when the special session met. In general structure the bill followed the lines of the Wisconsin act. It provided for a higher progressive rate (one to five per cent) on all income of residents, both individuals and corporations, and on the income of non-residents " derived from property located or business transacted within the state." The legislature repealed the law already on the statute books, but declined to pass the new bill. Instead it established a special revenue commission and required it " to inquire into and make recommendations as to the policy or necessity of the adoption of appropriate legislation of a system of taxation of incomes and the relation of such a system of taxation to the present system of taxation of property." The latter bill was approved by the governor, but the repeal of the existing tax law was vetoed. As a result

[1] New Mexico Special Revenue Commission, *Report*, 1920, p. 37.

the special revenue commission was given the task of passing upon the desirability of the adoption of a tax which was already adopted, and on the other hand some of the advantages which were expected from the continuance of the operation of the law failed to materialize. It was hoped that some important constitutional questions concerning the law might be settled. It proved that the act was universally disregarded and treated as a dead letter. Practically no returns were filed (although the penalty for failure to file was fine and imprisonment) and nothing was paid into the state treasury. The state treasurer did not at first issue the blanks for making returns on the ground that the funds to pay for such forms were to be drawn from the proceeds of a tax which in all likelihood would never be collected.

The special commission's report dealt first with the question of constitutionality. The commission noted the fact that in no state with a constitution similar to that of New Mexico had a progressive income tax been upheld.[1] On the other hand, it reached the conclusion that a law imposing a tax on incomes at a flat rate would be reasonably safe from attack on constitutional grounds. It held also that the classification of corporations by exclusion would be a justifiable measure. The commission expressed its belief that income could not be correctly classified as property.

The commission recommended a strictly personal income tax applying to the net income of every person within the state. The exemptions should be made exactly the same as those under the federal income tax law, not only because the federal exemptions are believed to be " essentially reasonable and just " but also on account of the administrative advantage of an effective check on evasion. The determination of taxable income should also follow along the

[1] New Mexico Special Revenue Commission, *Report*, 1920, p. 38 *et seq.*

lines of the federal tax. With regard to the question of
rates, the commission held that as long as the federal rates
remained at the existing high level, New Mexico was pre-
cluded from establishing a heavily progressive state income tax. The soundest considerations were those in-
dicating a low flat rate. This rate should not be more than
four per cent, and during the first year of administration
should not be more than two per cent. Using the statistics
of income compiled by the federal government, the commission concluded that a two per cent rate on 1920 incomes would bring in about $300,000.[1]

The commission considered that the " simplest and most
sensible " disposition of the yield would be to dedicate it
to the state school fund. In states where the localities have
been asked to surrender certain taxes as a condition to the
establishment of the income tax, it has usually proved advisable to apportion a share of the income tax receipts directly to the local authorities. In New Mexico no considerable sacrifices would be made by the counties and a direct apportionment would be unnecessary. The commission recommended that the state tax commission should be given
the administration of the income tax law.

In the opinion of the commission the establishment of a
personal income tax should be accompanied by the passage
of a law exempting intangible personal property from taxation. With an income tax, the owners of such intangibles
would be contributing to the support of the state. The
older system of personal property taxation has been a
lamentable failure in New Mexico, as it has elsewhere.

The commission's report was presented in November,
1920, and it was believed that the legislature of 1921 would
base legislation upon its recommendations. The commis-

[1] New Mexico Special Revenue Commission, *Report*, 1920, p. 50.

sion wisely took account of the fact that New Mexico is a state in which somewhat " primitive economic conditions " still prevail (the state paid only nine-hundredths of one per cent of the total federal income taxes paid for 1918) and framed its recommendations accordingly. However interesting the experiment in New Mexico may be, its experience cannot yet be of great value in guiding the wealthier industrial states in shaping their legislation.

2. *The attempt to introduce an income tax in Alabama*

In 1919-1920 the state of Alabama made its second experiment with an income tax law. The first income tax, which was levied from 1843 to 1884, began its existence as a tax on specified business incomes. In the course of its existence frequent revisions were made and the tax changed character almost completely. In 1844 the list of professions was enlarged, and in 1848 extended to include all professions and business except those of artisans and manual laborers. In 1850 the law was so modified that the professional income tax became partly a license tax. In 1862 the rates of the income tax were again increased and its application extended. Finally, in 1866 a general income tax of " one per cent . . . . upon the annual gains, profits, salaries, and income in excess of $500 received by any person within the state " was adopted.[1]

After the close of the Civil War the administration of the income tax degenerated rapidly. The yield decreased from about $11,000 out of a total state tax of $1,122,000 in 1870 to $8,100 in 1879.[2] At the same time the tax was becoming increasingly unpopular. As a result of the recommendations of the state auditor the provisions for levying

[1] D. O. Kinsman, *The Income Tax in the Commonwealths of the United States* (New York, 1903), p. 80.

[2] E. R. A. Seligman, *The Income Tax* (New York, 1914), p. 410.

the state tax were dropped, and after 41 years of existence the income tax of Alabama came to an end.

The law passed in 1919[1] represented one of a series of revenue reforms undertaken by the legislature of that year. A graduated tax was imposed upon the incomes of resident individuals and domestic corporations, and upon the income of non-resident individuals and foreign corporations arising within the state. The customary deductions were allowed. The sums of $1,000 for the individual, $2,000 for a married person or the head of a family, and $300 for each dependent, were allowed as exemptions. The income was was to be assessed at the following rates:

Net income	Rate (per cent)
In excess of $5,000	2
In excess of $5,000 but not in excess of $7,500	2½
In excess of $7,500 but not in excess of $10,000	3
In excess of $10,000 but not in excess of $15,000	3½
In excess of $15,000	4

The state tax commission, created under the terms of the same act, was given the duty of administering the law, and one of its members, to be known as the income tax supervisor, was to administer it. After deducting the commissions of the local collectors, 35 per cent of the proceeds of the tax were to go to the municipality of which the taxpayer was a resident, 25 per cent to the county, and the balance to the state. The form of the law, with its provision for graduated rates, central control, and the distribution of the proceeds, showed the influence of the successful measures of the few years preceding its enactment, and contained the promise of a far more effective income tax than that which Alabama abandoned in 1884.

The income tax law of 1919 was shortlived. On March

[1] *Laws of Alabama*, 1919, ch. 328.

20, 1920, its was held unconstitutional in the circuit court, on the ground that as a property tax it exceeded the constitutional limit of 65 cents per $100, and on the ground that it was discriminatory in character. This decision was affirmed by the state supreme court on April 24, 1920.[1]

Although New Mexico and Alabama are both relatively poor states with little modern industrial enterprise within their borders, the occasion for the experiments with the income tax is the same in each instance,—the omnipresent dissatisfaction with the property tax. The special commission in New Mexico called attention to the fact that even in that state where " the economic strength of the state is still largely implicit " personal property had almost entirely disappeared from the assessment rolls. The *amount* of such property which escapes taxation in such a state is small, relatively at least, but it is plainly the mark of prudence to recognize the situation as early as possible and to make the necessary changes in the revenue system. In these states the attempt has failed at first, for varying reasons, but in both cases there is evidence that the dissatisfaction with the old system has not been quieted and that fresh efforts for reform are to follow.

[1] *Bulletin of the National Tax Association,* vol. v, no. 8 (May, 1920), pp. 262, 263; vol. v, no. 9 (June, 1920), p. 292.

CHAPTER X

THE INCOME TAX MOVEMENT IN OTHER STATES

THE present period of interest in the taxation of personal incomes as a means of remedying the inequities of the personal property tax and of bringing about contributions to the expenses of the state from those best able to pay has not beeen confined to the states whose income tax measures have been described in the preceding chapters. In a number of other states, particularly in Ohio, Georgia, and California, the movement has attained considerable prominence and at times the adoption of the income tax has seemed imminent. In other states preliminary steps have been taken. In the following pages the most significant of these movements are described.

1. *Proposals for an income tax in Ohio*

The constitution of the state of Ohio contains provision for the adoption of an income tax,[1] but no active steps were taken in that direction until the state revenue system was submitted to scrutiny by a special committee in 1919. The General Assembly of 1919, which convened early in January, recognized at once the pressing nature of the financial problems before it. Both state and municipal treasuries were facing serious shortages at that time. Emergency measures were promptly enacted, a committee was appointed to recommend legislative measures for increasing the revenue, and a recess was taken in order to allow the

---

[1] *Constitution of Ohio*, art. ii, sec. 8.

committee time in which to do its work.   The committee, known as the Special Joint Taxation Committee of the 83rd Ohio General Assembly, rendered its report in December, 1919.   The new revenue measures recommended by the committee were an income tax, an inheritance tax, and a tax on motor vehicles.

During the course of the preparation of its income tax bill the committee made a study of the experience of those states which had had the best results with income taxes, particularly Wisconsin, Massachusetts, and New York. Use was also made of the plan for a model system of state and local taxation prepared by a committee of the National Tax Association (See Appendix I).   The bill provided that the tax should be imposed only upon the incomes of persons resident in the state, but that all income received by residents of the state, from whatever source derived, should be included in the return of income.   Professor Harley L. Lutz, economic adviser to the committee, comments as follows on the taxation of non-residents:[1]

The attempt to tax nonresidents upon the income from property owned and from business, trades, professions or occupations carried on in New York was inspired by a local situation which has no parallel in Ohio.   A large number of persons do business or earn incomes in New York and reside in New Jersey, and the tax on nonresidents was confessedly aimed at this group.   The taxation of nonresidents is not approved by the committee on a model tax system, and its argument against the practice is familiar to this committee.

The definition of gross income in the committee's bill followed closely that contained in the federal law.   Stock dividends were excluded from taxable income.   The deductions for the purpose of determining taxable net income

[1] H. L. Lutz, " The Operation of State Income Taxes," *Report of the (Ohio) Special Joint Taxation Committee,* p. 107 of the report.

followed those of the federal law. The exemptions were set at $500 for unmarried persons and $1,000 for married persons, with $200 additional for each dependent. The committee recognized the fact that these limits were unusually low:[1]

We recognize that these figures mean an encroachment upon that subsistence minimum which all authorities agree should be exempted, but we have ventured thus far because of our desire to secure as wide a diffusion of the burden of the income tax as possible, and also because of the need of additional revenue from the tax.

The committee considered the possibility of requiring taxpayers to file a copy of their federal returns upon which the state income tax might be applied, but decided against it on several grounds. First, the conflict of tax jurisdictions would involve complications; second, there were other differences in the determination of gross and net income; and third, it seemed desirable from the administrative standpoint of the state to have a separate return made, so that the state authorities might have complete control over a set of returns.

The bill placed the state tax commission in general charge of the income tax, and enlarged the commission for that purpose. The county auditor was made local collector of incomes, ex-officio, and was to appoint deputies and other assistants. Returns were to be made to the county auditors. The county auditor was to make the assessment, and the tax was to be collected by the county treasurer " at the same time and in the same manner as other taxes." The tax commission was empowered to require information at the source.

[1] *Report,* p. 75.

The rates of taxation to be applied were as follows:

Taxable income	Rate (per cent)
First $4,000	1
Above $4,000	2

The committee took advantage of the material on the status of incomes in the various states through the publication of *Statistics of Income for 1917* by the United States income tax authorities, and prepared a careful statement of the yield of the tax on incomes above $2,000. Taken together with the estimates of the probable yield of the tax on incomes below that amount, the probable yield of the total tax was estimated at from $7,000,000 to $8,000,000.

The proposed distribution of the proceeds was in the ratio of three-fourths to the municipal corporations and townships in which the funds originated, and one-fourth to the state to become part of the general revenue. This provision gave recognition not only to the constitutional requirement in Ohio that 50 per cent of the collection of such taxes must be returned to the source, but also to the great needs of the cities. The well-known fact that the income tax has always proved to be an urban tax was noted, and it was anticipated that from the apportionment to the localities of about $6,000,000 of the estimated yield in the first year of the collection of the tax the cities would obtain some relief from the serious financial difficulties under which they were laboring at the time when the commission was doing its work, although the relief for the year 1920 would still be inadequate.

The income tax bill was promptly defeated by both branches of the legislature when it was introduced in December, 1919.[1] The basis of opposition was the argument

[1] *Bulletin of the National Tax Association,* vol. v, no. 5 (Feb., 1920), p. 133.

that such a law must necessarily contain inquisitorial provisions which would disclose intangible property to the
taxing officials, with the result that it would thenceforward
be subject to taxation, and the arguments of banks and other
financial institutions that serious injuries to their business
would follow the passage of such an act. Repeated attempts were made to pass the bill with amendments covering
some of the points under objection, but all hope of its
ultimate passage was finally abandoned late in December,
1919.

2. *The income tax movement in Georgia*

In Georgia a recent attempt to introduce a personal income tax has failed, although the evidence indicates that the
movement had and probably still has the force of a considerable body of public opinion behind it. Georgia had
had one rather unusual experience with the personal income tax at the time of the Civil War.[1] In 1863 a tax on
profits was levied, with a progressive rate based on the
ratio of income to capital, and so planned that—theoretically at least—if profits were ten time capital the entire
income went as taxes. Evasion and fraud very naturally
resulted, and the tax was dropped soon after the war.

The late attempt to introduce an income tax drew its
support from a knowledge of the increasing use of the personal income tax in other states. In Georgia, as in other
states, Civil War experiments are recognized to have little
value in dealing with twentieth-century fiscal problems.
In 1918 the legislature found the state's sources of revenue
inadequate to provide funds for the ever-increasing government expenses and at the same time it realized the seriousness of the restrictions upon the taxing power found in the

[1] Seligman *op. cit.*, pp. 411, 412.

state constitution. A special tax commission was at once appointed to investigate the state's tax system and to compare it with that of other states and countries. This committee, reporting in 1919, suggested several important changes in the system, and included in its recommendations a proposal for a constitutional amendment permitting the imposition of income and inheritance taxes with graduated rates. The committee described its position as follows: [1]

Recognizing, as we do, that an income tax is perhaps the fairest and most equitable method of raising revenue, particularly from those classes of property which are the most difficult to assess, we are pleased to note that Congress has enacted a law which gives those states having an income tax law, upon the request of the Governor of the State, access to the data upon which the federal income tax is now assessed, so far as it affects corporations, and we hope that a similar provision will soon be made in that affecting the income of individuals.

The only reasonable objections to taxation by this method being the difficulty and expense attending its administration, and both of these having been entirely eliminated by the granting of the privilege mentioned above, we recommend that Georgia get in line by enacting, as soon as the Constitutional amendment hereinbefore provided for will permit, a law providing for taxation on an income basis, and at a very low rate.

The proposed legislation received a favorable report from the committee on constitutional amendments of the legislature of 1919, but action was deferred until the 1920 session. In the summer session of 1920 a bill providing for a constitutional amendment authorizing the levy and collection of an income tax was passed by the House of Representatives but failed of passage in the Senate. If passed, the proposal was to have been submitted to the voters at the election in November, 1920. The failure of the bill in the legislature of 1920 means that a considerable period

[1] (Georgia) Special Tax Commission, *Report*, 1919, p. 43.

must elapse before a personal income tax bill can again be passed by the legislature and the proposal ratified by the people.

3. *The income tax movement in California*

The agitation for an income tax in California was only temporarily quieted by the presentation of an unfavorable commission report in 1906. After the Wisconsin experience demonstrated the practicability of an income tax of a new kind the interest in the tax in California increased. Bills providing for a personal income tax have reached several legislatures but have failed of passage. In late years one of the most earnest advocates of the adoption of the tax has been Mr. Clifton E. Brooks, member of the legislature for Oakland. Mr. Brooks stated his position in the *California Taxpayers' Journal* in September, 1919:[1]

The income tax for the state will not be an experiment. In Wisconsin it is producing annually a revenue of $2,000,000 and in Massachusetts $12,000,000 from sources that previously escaped taxation for the most part. In population and wealth, California ranks about half-way between Wisconsin and Massachusetts. It would not be a matter of too abundant optimism to estimate the revenue that California could develop from this source at $6,000,- 000. . . .

The income tax is also desirable because it will provide an opportunity to abolish, at a later date, present crude, inefficient and unjust methods of taxing (1) Personal Property and (2) Corporation Franchises. All assessors regard the present method of taxing personal property as the " joke " tax. When the income tax is established, taxes paid upon personal property should be deducted for awhile, as the income tax would be used solely to hunt out the " personal property tax slacker " as before stated. When it could be demonstrated that the income tax was the most efficient method of raising public revenue from this source, then the

---

[1] C. E. Brooks, " Shall we have an Income Tax?", *California Taxpayers' Journal,* vol. iii, no. 7 (Sept., 1919), pp. 12, 13.

logical step would be to abolish the personal property tax. It should, perhaps, be mentioned at this point that rates in connection with a state income tax would be very low. The federal tax produces in California $76,000,000. Since the amount which it would be desirable to raise from this source would be only about a twelfth or thirteenth, the rate need be but a fraction of the federal rate.

Mr. Brooks introduced a bill embodying his opinions in the legislature of 1921, as the first bill presented. Every individual and corporation subject to the federal income tax was included under the terms of the proposed legislation. The net income arrived at in the federal return less the tax paid to the United States and income received from investments without the state would be the net income for the purposes of determining the amount of the tax due. The rates of the proposed tax were as follows:

Taxable income	*Rate (per cent)*
First $10,000	1
Next $40,000	2
Above $50,000	3

The proposed measure against the judgment of some of the persons interested in its passage, failed to provide for exempting intangible personal property from taxation. Income derived from sources within the state was exempted. Opposition to the bill developed at once, and the assumed high cost of collection received considerable emphasis. It was also urged that the tax would be inquisitorial in character.

4. *Other steps towards income taxes*

For a number of years New Hampshire has been included in the list of states in which the question of an income tax is under consideration. The constitutional convention assembled in June, 1918, took up the question of an in-

come tax amendment, but the convention found it necessary
to postpone all of its business until after the close of the
war.   In January, 1920, the convention met again.   It was
recommended that the income tax amendment be referred
to the people in the election of November, 1920.

At that time New Hampshire was greatly in need of increased revenue and the unprecedented increase in local assessments made it appear that the taxes on tangible property were nearing the " limit of endurance." [1]   Nevertheless the income tax amendment, together with six others,
was defeated in the election of November, 1920.   It was
believed by the supporters of the amendment that the consideration which these measures would ordinarily have received was lacking on account of the intense interest in the
presidential election.   The constitutional convention was
expected to reconvene in 1921 and to submit the amendment
to the voters again.   The situation in New Hampshire appears to promise well for the introduction of the income
tax if the matter is brought up a second time.

The proposal for an income tax in Minnesota has had an
almost similar fate.   The legislature of 1919 voted to submit an income tax to the people at the next election.   The
amendment provided that " taxes may be imposed on privileges and occupations, which taxes may be graduated and
progressive and the exemption of a reasonable amount of
income from taxation may be provided, and such taxes may
be in lieu of taxes on any class or classes of personal property as the legislature may determine."   The amendment
failed of passage in the November elections.

A number of other states are taking up the question of
income taxes.   Indiana has adopted a constitutional amend-

---

[1] A. O. Brown, " The Taxation of Incomes under the New Hampshire
Constitution," *Bulletin of the National Tax Association,* vol. iv, no. 5
(Feb., 1919), p. 121.

ment providing for the tax.   In Maine and Oregon the matter has come up repeatedly, only to be defeated.   New bills failed of passage in Kansas and in Utah in 1921.   Most important of all, New Jersey has called for the presentation to the legislature of 1922 of a bill providing for a state income tax on a sliding scale.   If a third great industrial state follows New York and Massachusetts, the spread of the movement throughout the eastern states is probable.

CHAPTER XI

Modern Income Tax Methods and Results

In the course of a decade of development of state taxation of incomes the characteristics of this type of tax in the United States have become fairly well-defined. On the whole the taxes on personal incomes have been introduced in the form and manner most immediately practicable, without the accompaniment of plans for a coherent tax system. The majority of the state income-tax laws and rulings which now appear so highly complex have " just growed " like the famous little negress of fiction. We look in vain for a debate on " graduation " of the type which occurred repeatedly in the English House of Commons from the middle of the nineteenth century until early in the twentieth when an extensively graduated scale of taxation for individual incomes was adopted. " Differentiation " between earned and unearned incomes, which has been produced in two states by employing different rates of taxation for funded and unfunded incomes, has been introduced with little realization of the complicated principles involved or of the possible perversity of state revenues under the plan. Systems of exemptions and deductions have grown up which bear a rough resemblance to those devised for the federal income tax law but which are still in a confused state. Double taxation, rapidly becoming a pressing problem, has been almost ignored except in a few instances. Administrative methods have been recognized as important from the beginning of the decade, and although there are still backward states, several effective organizations have been built up.

1. *Income tax rates*

The policies of the American states with regard to progression are in a chaotic condition. Seven of the states imposed graduated rates upon personal incomes at the beginning of 1921. No two of these systems were alike. At one extreme was Virginia, with a rate of one per cent on the first $3,000 of taxable income and two per cent on the remainder, and at the other was North Dakota, with 23 separate rates. reaching a maximum of 10 per cent on earned incomes of more than $40,000. The degree of progression employed appears to have varied inversely with the desire of the state legislators to fit the personal income tax inconspicuously into the existing state and federal systems, and directly with the desire to extract a considerable portion of the state revenues from individuals in possession of large fortunes.

The arguments for and against progression are simple. Since the surplus over and above the amount required for the necessaries of life increases more rapidly than additions to total income, persons at the higher income levels are able to pay relatively large amounts towards the support of the government under which they live than those with smaller incomes. An ability theory of taxation consequently demands the progressive taxation of personal incomes. Only by adhering to a benefit theory of taxation can a progressive rate for this type of tax be opposed. The chief complicating factor in the United States is the existence of a federal income tax which reaches an extremely high rate on the largest incomes. When the richest individuals in the country are already paying into the federal treasury amounts corresponding to 73 per cent on a part of the income received, even the most ardent advocate of contribution according to ability is satisfied. The absorption of any considerable part of the remainder by any government whatsoever might properly be regarded as approaching confiscation. The state governments, therefore, must take into account the fact that individuals taxed by them are already paying into the national exchequer amounts graded with the intention of exacting contributions in accordance with ability to pay, and must be on their guard lest the carefully devised federal plan be distorted through the operation of the state tax.

The weight of argument at the present time is on the side of a mildly progressive tax, not rising above six per cent, for the use of the states. A tax of this kind is plainly in accord with the principles of ability taxation, and at the same time the maximum is so low that the intentions of the federal tax framers are not seriously interfered with. If the state income tax is imposed at a proportional rate, even though this rate is fixed at a point which produces a large return, the burden of the tax upon the persons in receipt of small incomes is relatively so much heavier than upon the well-to-do that a general and merited dissatisfaction with the state income tax is likely to result.

Differentiation between earned and unearned incomes for purposes of taxation, with the imposition of a higher rate upon the latter, has received far less attention in this country than in England. In Massachusetts the taxation of income from intangibles at six per cent while business incomes are taxed at one and one-half per cent [1] is the result of an attempt to distinguish earned from unearned incomes. The rates employed in the taxation of income from intangibles are unusually heavy in comparison with those

---

[1] Exclusive of emergency additions to the rates.

on business incomes. In North Dakota the rates on the lower amounts of unearned income are only double those on similar amounts of earned income and the distinction disappears after $40,000 is reached. No other state accomplishes differentiation by direct means, and in the federal system the distinction between the two types of income is ignored. In England differentiation was recognized as a desirable principle and introduced to a minor extent in 1907. In subsequent years the scheme was elaborated until five different rates were applied to earned incomes below the point of £2,500, at which the full normal rate was put into effect. At the present time the trend of opinion in England is in the direction of diminishing the amount of differentiation employed. The Royal Commission on the Income Tax which reported in 1920 held that differentiation had been carried too far and that the devices employed operated unjustly with respect to certain classes of taxpayers. The Commission noted the general impression that small unearned income (or "investment" incomes, as the Commission preferred to call them) which were derived mainly from investment of savings out of earned income were harshly treated, and suggested as a remedy for this and other evils of the differentiation plan the simple device of diminishing earned incomes by one-tenth for purposes of taxation.[1]

Much of the sentiment in the United States is against differentiation, for the present at least. A strong argument for such a division of personal incomes may be framed from the point of view of abstract justice. If taxation is to be utilized as a means of administering rewards to the deserving, the individual actively engaged in a business or profession should be handled lightly as compared with

[1] Royal Commission on the Income Tax, *Report,* 1920, part ii, paragraphs 109, 110 (p. 25).

the unproductive member of society. Moreover, the recipient of a *large* investment income has, potentially or actually, a greater ability to pay than the recipient of an equivalent amount of earned income, since the productive powers of the recipient of investment income are presumably unemployed or employed in another direction. The possessors of *small* investment incomes are probably in many cases in quite another situation. The available evidence in England shows that this class is composed to so great an extent of "widow-and-orphan" members and their kind, incapable of becoming producers, that the payment of income taxes at any but a nominal rate is liable to result in real hardship.

A difficulty of another kind presented itself early in the history of the tax in North Dakota, where it was found that the amount of unearned income received in the state was unexpectedly small, and the revenue from the tax on that income correspondingly insignificant. It is in such communities as this, where agriculture is of prime importance and industries are relatively undeveloped, that the accumulation of capital is most in need of encouragement. From the point of view of obtaining funds for the extension of both agriculture and industry, the discovery of North Dakota that the unearned income derived within its borders was small in amount was a significant indication that one of the pressing needs of the state was the accumulation of its own capital, and that efforts to develop that capital should not be unduly discouraged.

If state income taxes are to form a part of such a system as that advocated by the Committee on Model Taxation, in which the personal income tax supplements a business tax and a tax upon tangible personal property, there is additional taxation upon the sources from which investment or funded incomes are derived, and attempts at further differentiation may be unnecessary. Differentiation produced in this way seems easier of accomplishment at the present time, especially from the administrative point of view, than that brought about by applying two separate scales of rates. It is also probably less onerous in its effects upon the recipients of small unearned incomes than the methods now employed in Massachusetts and North Dakota. Possibly the time will come when such a plan as that which has been suggested in England, the diminishing of earned income by one-tenth for purposes of taxation, will seem both practicable and just; but before that step is taken the incidence of the tax upon tangible property as employed in the United States should be determined as accurately as possible and carefully described, so that the amount of differentiation effected through that means alone may be clearly understood.

2. *Exemptions and deductions*

State income taxes, like the federal income tax, are ordinarily computed with reference to a number of exemptions and deductions. These two terms are used with little strictness in some of the less carefully framed state laws, but it is usually understood that the word " exemptions " should be applied to those parts of *income* which are not subject to taxation on account of individual and family responsibilities and to other kinds of income, such as the proceeds of life insurance policies and interest on bonds of the United States, which for a variety of reasons should be left out of account in ascertaining the gross income of the taxpayer; while the term " deductions " should be applied to those subtractions from the gross income received which are permitted on account of *expenditures* incurred for such purposes as carrying on business and the payment of taxes. The term " offset " is used merely to indicate the credit given on the taxpayer's bill, in a few states only, for other taxes paid. This credit has been limited almost without exception to one for personal property tax payments.

The *amounts* of personal income exempted from taxation under the various state laws show a great lack of uniformity, and the *nature* of the exemptions permitted exemplifies in another way the chaotic condition of income tax principles in this country. Attempts to follow the federal scheme of exemptions have been made in every state in which general income tax laws have been passed since 1913, the date of the first federal income-tax law, but on account of later changes in the federal law the results have been confusing. The first federal law provided for the exemption of $3,000 for the individual or $4,000 if the taxpayer was a married person and living with the spouse. In 1916 a further allowance of $200 for each child was granted to the head of a family. When the law was amended in 1917 for the purpose of providing additional war revenue the exemptions were lowered to $1,000 for single and $2,000 for married persons. In 1918 the credit of $200 for each child was extended to cover other dependents.

The income tax laws of Wisconsin and Mississippi, which were adopted before the enactment of a federal income tax law, illustrate the differences of terms which are in part responsible for the varying degrees of success with which state income tax laws have met. In Wisconsin the personal exemptions were fixed at $800 for single and $1,200 for married persons, with $200 for each dependent. These amounts are now considered remarkably low, particularly in view of the price changes which have since some about, but they were originally fixed with great care and with a view of obtaining direct personal contributions toward the expenses of state and local government from every citizen of taxpaying ability. The Mississippi exemption limit

was fixed at $2,500, without regard to the marital status of
the taxpayer, showing a lack of consideration for taxpaying
ability which was certain to create dissatisfaction. By 1915
the federal law was in operation, and Oklahoma naturally
adopted its plan of exemptions in the essentials, although
Oklahoma increased the child exemption to $500 in the
case of persons engaged solely in acquiring an education.
According to the Massachusetts law, passed in 1916, business incomes were distinguished from three other types of
income and taxed separately. Possibly for this reason a new
set of exemptions, $2,000, $2,500, and $250 additional for
children under 18, was chosen in that state.   Missouri's first
law, in 1917, followed along the federal lines, necessitating
a change to lower exemptions when the federal law was
revised, a change which Missouri made in 1919.   The
second state which passed a personal income tax law in
1917, Delaware, at first specified merely $1,000 as the in-
dividual exemption, without regard to the marital condition of the taxpayer, but the state law was changed to
correspond to the federal law in 1919.   In the relatively
unimportant revisions which were made by Virginia in
1918 and North Carolina in 1919, it was apparently not
considered necessary to change the exemptions to correspond with those of the federal law.   The new laws passed
in 1919, which uniformly follow the federal system of personal exemptions, reflect the spread of the realization that
the federal exemptions are reasonable and workable and
that a failure to conform to them introduces an unnecessary
complication in the administration of the various laws.
These new laws were those of New York, North Dakota,
and New Mexico.   The Alabama law which was passed in
the same year but was subsequently declared unconstitutional was constructed along the same lines with the exception of the fact that $300 instead of $200 was allowed
for each dependent.

The differences in the amounts of personal income exempted in the various states result in a variation of the tax burden which in its effect is like that of an actual difference in rates of taxation upon small incomes. Two steps which are immediately desirable are the lowering of the limits in several of the states and a movement in the direction of greater uniformity. The Committee on a Model System of State and Local Taxation, which is working for uniformity along with an adaptation of state and local systems of taxation to present-day economic conditions, embodied in its preliminary report the suggestion that $600 for single persons and $1,200 for married persons, with $200 for each dependent, with a possible total limited to $1,800, were the maximum exemptions which should be granted (September, 1918). The principal reasons for suggesting the taxation of incomes smaller than those taxed by any of the states at the time when the report was made was the committee's conviction that under a democratic form of government as few people as possible should be exempted from the necessity of making a direct personal contribution towards the support of the state. In the draft of a personal income tax law which the same committee published two and one-half years later [1] the exemptions were set at $1,000 and $2,000, with $200 additional for each dependent, like those of the federal income tax law. In view of the condition of affairs in the United States with regard to state and federal income taxes, the later decision of the committee contains the more workable exemptions. It is true, as the committee urged in its preliminary report, that a democratic form of government implies direct personal responsibility for support on the part of all who

[1] *Bulletin of the National Tax Association,* vol, vi, no. 4 (Jan., 1921), pp. 102-112.

are able to contribute. It as also true, as the British Royal Commission which investigated the subject of a low exemption limit in Great Britain in 1919 was forcefully informed, that a low exemption limit for personal income taxes makes possible light taxes in other forms which affect the same class of people. Moreover, a high exemption of personal incomes operates so that many sections and localities pay almost no income tax, and sectional and class antagonisms are correspondingly intensified. At the same time the effort to make the exemptions so low that all persons with taxpaying ability contribute to the government under which they live should not be carried so far that the result is the taxation of persons who are already at the minimum-of-subsistence level.

It is plain that the exemptions permitted by the federal law are not high, especially in view of the recent changes in the price levels for necessities. The individual exemption of $1,000 corresponds to $500 or $600 before the outbreak of the European War. The imposition of an income tax on amounts less than $1,000 would almost certainly arouse dissatisfaction with the tax which would more than cancel the rather vague benefits of forcing persons with low incomes to make direct contributions to the support of the government under which they live. Whatever tax burden is carried by the poorest people in the various cities and states is carried almost unconsciously, and no theoretical justification of direct taxpaying would be acceptable. The vote of the South Wales miners against the low exemption limit retained in Great Britain through 1919, a time of rapidly rising costs, is a case in point.

The cost of collection of the taxes on small incomes, taxes which are actually nominal in character, is another point which should be taken into consideration. Figures for the cost of collection on the various classes of income are not available in this country, for either federal or state taxes; but an estimate to the effect that one-half of the collections on the incomes just above $1,000 are eaten up by administrative expenses might prove to be correct.

Although a large proportion of the federal income tax receipts come from the Middle Atlantic and New England states, the federal exemptions are so low that little actual regional immunity from the operation of the income tax exists. It is difficult and unsatisfactory to attempt to fix a point on the scale of incomes which means the avoidance of the irritation and expense of very low exemptions and at the same time freedom from the sectional and class distinctions of high exemptions, but in view of all the issues, $1,000 and $2,000, as permitted under the federal law, seem fairly satisfactory. From the point of view of administration the advantages of uniformity are great. If the same individuals are taxable under state and federal laws, the returns are made with less confusion to the taxpayer, and greater opportunity for getting accurate results and detecting evasion on the part of the state administration.

If the tendency towards uniformity in exemptions which showed itself in the state income tax legislation of 1919 continues, many of the inequalities of tax burden on those with small incomes will be wiped out. These inequalities are most conspicious when the three states which have made the greatest financial success of the income tax are compared. New York, with its similarity to the federal system, Massachusetts with the separate taxation of four kinds of income and a high exemption limit for business incomes, and Wisconsin with an unusually low exemption limit, illustrate the haphazard manner in which the state taxes have developed. In Wisconsin, where the general payment of the income tax by all classes of citizens has been accepted with a fair degree of equanimity, there is already talk of a change.

The tax commission of that state reports that " there is warrant for an increase in the family exemptions under present economic conditions," [1] but refrains from urging it or recommending it to the legislature.

A tendency on the part of the states to recognize an obligation to encourage education is beginning to show itself in the terms of the exemption provisions. Oklahoma, which ordinarily allows $200 to the taxpayer for each person dependent upon him, increases the sum to $500 in cases in which " such dependent is engaged solely in acquiring an education." The Massachusetts tax commissioner, in his report for 1919, called attention to the fact that the age limit of 18 for children for whom exemption might be claimed, while desirable from an administrative point of view, operated harshly against moderately circumstanced merchants and relatively low-salaried professional men who were financing one or more boys or girls through a college course. The commissioner suggested the consideration of an age limit of 21 for this reason, and promised the presentation of statistics showing the effect of such a change upon the revenue.

The question of greater flexibility in family exemption has received little attention in this country. In view of the thorough-going attempts which have been made to make due allowance for the various ways in which business expenses are incurred and the various forms in which they may appear, it is not unlikely that a corresponding attempt may soon be made to allow for the vicissitudes of family life. A beginning was made when the exemptions for dependents under the Wisconsin law were made contingent in each case upon the dependent's being " actually supported and entirely dependent " upon the taxpayer for his support. [2]

---

[1] *Report*, 1920, p. 42.

[2] *Laws of Wisconsin*, 1913, ch. 720.

That is, the state of affairs within the family with regard to actual support was taken into consideration in the computation of the tax. Oklahoma's enlargement of the exemption from $200 to $500 " while such dependent is engaged solely in acquiring an education " is a second step, marking as it does a legal recognition of the way in which the energies of the dependent are used and the expenses for which the taxpayer may be expected to become liable on his account, as well as the degree of dependency. Another step might conceivably be the extension of exemptions or, rather, the allowance of deductions for extraordinary expenses incurred for reasons other than acquiring an education, such as serious or prolonged illness. Another possibility is that of allowing exemptions for persons *partially* dependent for support upon the taxpayer. The general impression among the taxpayers with small incomes that taxpayers who *share* the burden of the support of aged parents, for example, are unjustly discriminated against in favor of those who bear the whole burden of dependents will almost certainly find some reflection in future legislation.

Several other classes of exemptions have been permitted under the various state income tax laws, but with even less uniformity than the family exemptions. Massachusets exemptions from the operation of the personal income tax dividends from Massachusetts corporations, income from real estate wherever situated, and interest on deposits in Massachusetts savings banks. Wisconsin and New Mexico accomplish the same result in a more limited way by exempting income from the securities of corporations which pay an income tax to the state. Inheritances proper are usually exempted, although the income from the property represented is ordinarily taxable. Life insurance payments and amounts received from workmen's compensation awards are also ordinarily exempt.

One of the most puzzling questions which has been involved in the determination of net income, and a question which is for that reason closely associated with that of proper exemptions, is concerned with the treatment of stock dividends. Beginning in 1916 the federal laws required the inclusion of stock dividends in gross income, an example which was followed by the states. Economists have generally agreed that the receipt for a stock dividend is not the receipt of an additional amount of income, but is merely a change in the form of the recipient's capital.[1]

According to a decision of the United States Supreme Court rendered on March 8, 1920,[2] a *bona fide* stock dividend is not " income " within the meaning of the Sixteenth Amendment. The definition of income adopted by the court, namely " income may be defined as the gain derived from capital, from labor or from both combined, provided it would be understood to include profit gained through the sale or conversion of assets " was interpreted by the court to exclude " a growth or increment of value in the investment." The decision was reached by a vote of five to four. Federal and state laws and administration were adjusted as rapidly as possible so as to conform to the decision, and as a result stock dividends are not now noted on income tax returns as a part of gross income.

All of the states allow numerous deductions from gross income in the determination of net taxable income. These deductions are coming more and more to conform to those permitted under the federal income tax legislation. The

[1] E. R. A. Seligman, " Are Stock Dividends Income?", *American Economic Review*, vol. ix, no. 3 (Sept., 1919), p. 517; F. R. Fairchild, " The Stock Dividends Decision," *Bulletin of the National Tax Association*, vol. v, no. 7 (April, 1920), p. 209.

[2] Eisner *v.* Macomber, United States Supreme Court, no. 318—October Term, 1919 (March 8, 1920), 40 Sup. Ct. 189.

most common items are those for the expenses of carrying
on the taxpayer's business or profession. These expenses
are ordinarily defined to include wages and salaries paid,
repairs, depreciation allowances, and all other ordinary and
necessary expenses for the maintenace of the taxpayer's
business, as well as losses and worthless debts. Interest
on indebtedness and all taxes paid to any taxing jurisdiction
may be deducted in most states. In New York and Wisconsin gifts to educational, charitable, religious, and certain
other non-commercial organizations, to the amount of not
more than 15 per cent of the taxpayer's net income may
also be deducted,—a provision which was patterned after
one included in the federal income tax law.

The deduction permitted on account of gifts made during the year opens the way for further deductions with reference to the uses to which the taxpayer's income is put.
There are gifts other than those to recognized charitable,
educational, and religious institutions and organizations
which may be made without intent to lighten the burden
of the income tax. For example, contributions to the support of political parties may have a purpose somewhat
similar to that of gifts to charitable organizations.

In recent years the desirability of limiting in some way
the deductions allowable for interest on indebtedness has
received a considerable amount of attention. The preliminary report of the Committee on Model Taxation shows
a recognition of the change in the form of taxable income
which results from the issue by the federal government of
large amounts of tax-exempt bonds, and contains a suggestion for the limitation of the interest deduction to an amount
proportional to the income derived from taxable sources. In
the words of the report "if a person derives one-half of
his income from taxable sources and one-half from tax-
exempt federal bonds, he should be permitted to deduct only

one-half of the interest which he pays on his indebtedness." [1]
This provision was omitted in the draft of a model personal
income tax law which the same committee published in
January, 1921. In the model law the deduction of "in-
erest paid during the income year on indebtedness" is
recommended without any qualifications whatsoever. In
the original New York law a provision almost identical
with that in the preliminary report appeared,[2] but this was
amended in the following year so as to permit simply the
deduction of "all interest paid or accrued during the taxable year on indebtedness.[3] While it may prove necessary
and desirable to limit in some way the amount of interest
on indebtedness which is deductible, it was to be expected
that the provisions noted above which related the amount
deductible to taxable income should prove unsatisfactory and
unpopular. The proportion of income derived from tax-
exempt sources obviously cannot be calculated until after
all deductions are made.

The kinds and amounts of taxes deductible under the laws
of the various states are very nearly the same. The ordinary procedure is to allow the deduction of all taxes (excluding special assessments) paid to any jurisdiction. Wisconsin does not allow the deduction of taxes on unproductive property, Mississippi allows the deduction of ad
valorem taxes only, and Oklahoma and Virginia do not
allow the deduction of taxes paid to the United States or to
foreign governments. New York allows the deduction of
all taxes except income taxes. With the deduction of taxes
as with many other matters connected with the personal income tax, the simplest plan is at the same time the most

[1] *Preliminary Report*, p. 15.
[2] *Laws of New York*, 1919, ch. 627, sec. 360, par. 2.
[3] *Laws of New York*, 1920, ch. 693.

equitable. The allowance of deductions for all taxes paid
to any jurisdiction is by far the best procedure. An attempt to tax amounts paid out as taxes may seriously affect the justice with which the whole scheme of taxation
operates if the rates are as heavy as income tax rates of
recent years have tended to become. For example, a tax
upon amounts paid into the federal treasury as income taxes
by an individual who receives an income of more than
$1,000,000 annually has an effect not contemplated and
probably not desired by the framers either of the federal or
the state income tax laws. A point of view very close to
this is taken by the Committee on Model Taxation, which incorporated in the draft of a model income tax law, a provision allowing the deduction of all taxes paid to the
United States or to any state or foreign country, with the
exception of inheritance taxes and income taxes paid in
the state of residence.

The question of offsets is closely connected with the
question of exemptions and deductions. The recent history
of state income taxes furnishes only two kinds of examples
of offsets, those for personal property taxes paid (permitted
in Wisconsin, North Dakota, and New Mexico) and those
for all property taxes paid (permitted for a short period in
Missouri). The undesirability of allowing these offsets has
been demonstrated. The Wisconsin tax commission has
for a number of years earnestly besought the legislature to
do away with the offset provision in that state and so to increase the revenue due from the income tax and abolish
various uncontemplated inequities. The offset as it is used
in Wisconsin subtracts nearly one-half of the income tax
revenue and defeats the purpose of the income tax in
principle. The Missouri provision was adapted from that
used in Wisconsin and was apparently suggested by it, but
it became unpopular early in its career and it was abolished

in 1919. The North Dakota law has been in operation for
only a short time, in the course of which more serious defects have caught the public attention, but there is no doubt
that the offset will prove to be out of place in that state in
the same way in which it has proved to be unsatisfactory
in other states. The New Mexico law is still to be tried
out. In states in which such a provision is in operation the
attempt of the framers of the personal income tax laws to
reach taxpaying ability in a more accurate fashion than was
possible under the older personal property tax laws is defeated, and the purposes which it was hoped to accomplish
through the distribution of the proceeds of the personal income tax are hindered to an extent corresponding to that
to which the offset is utilized.

A much more reasonable and workable provision is that
contained in the New York income tax law which allows
credit to non-residents of New York on the income tax bill
payable to New York state for income taxes paid in the
state or country of residence. The New York comptroller
credits the amount of tax payable by such non-resident
in New York state with such proportion of the income tax
payable by him elsewhere as his income subject to taxation
in New York state bears to his entire income upon which
the tax payable to the other state or country is imposed.[1]
This credit is allowed only if the state or country taxing the
non-resident grants a substantially similar credit to residents of New York subject to income taxation under that
laws of that state or country, or if the state or country taxes
the income of its own residents but exempts from taxation
the personal incomes of residents of New York state. This
provision represents an attempt to install a scheme of
reciprocity in crediting income taxes paid which will become

---

[1] *Laws of New York*, 1920, ch. 691.

more and more necessary as surrounding industrial states undertake the taxation of personal incomes. Such a plan should ultimately become unnecessary, however, if the state taxation of incomes becomes general and if the states follow the more equitable and reasonable method of taxing *residents only,* as recommended by the Committee on Model Taxation. The New York plan is merely an attempt to insure a fair distribution of the tax burden under present conditions and those of the immediate future.

3. *Double taxation*

The difficulties which arise from conflicts of tax jurisdiction are an old story in the United States, where the administration of the general property tax has been complicated by the fact that personal property is supposed to be taxed in the place of the taxpayer's domicile, but where the states in various instances have adopted conflicting procedures. The introduction of the taxation of personal incomes by the states has produced a new set of complications which are more troublesome than the old. In the words of Professor Seligman, "the possible combinations are almost terrifying in their complexity." [1]

A man might reside in one state, his legal domicile might be in a second state, his income might be derived from railroad securities which may be in a safe deposit vault in a third state; the railway itself may have its chief office in a fourth state, and its track may traverse several other states. Where and how should this income be taxed?

The regulation of double taxation is not without precedent. By the terms of the Prussian law of 1909 [2] the disadvantages of double taxation were minimized by provid-

[1] E. R. A. Seligman, *The Income Tax* (New York, 1914), pp. 647, 648.
[2] Seligman, *op. cit.,* p. 270.

ing that when trade or industry was carried on in several states only a proportional part of the income could be taxed in any one state. Legislation of this kind on the part of the federal government in the United States is hardly conceivable, and the necessary adaptations will undoubtedly have to be brought about through state agreements as to uniformity and by following the suggestions of such organizations as the National Tax Association's committee on a model system of state and local taxation.

The provisions of the Massachusetts law under which income from Massachusetts corporations and from deposits in savings banks and all income from real estate wherever situated is exempt from taxation under the laws taxing personal incomes represent an attempt to clear the commonwealth of Massachusetts itself from the onus of taxing the same income twice. The result is an unsatisfactory state of affairs with regard to income derived from sources outside the state. The assumption is that since the income of corporations and savings-bank deposits are taxed separately by Massachusetts, such income need not be taxed again in the hands of the recipient. A tax known as a " franchise tax " or a " tax upon the corporate excess " (i. e., total value of the capital stock less deductions allowed by law) is levied upon Massachusetts corporations, with the addition of a tax of two and one-half per cent upon net income as returned to the federal government. In the case of Massachusetts savings banks the tax is assessed upon average deposits less certain specified investments at the rate of two and one-half mills on the dollar.

The intention of the state of Massachusetts to refrain from taxing such incomes twice over is justifiable, and the operation of the law as it applies to resident individuals with respect to their interests in domestic corporations is easily understood. The complications arise with reference

to the taxation of income derived from foreign corporations.   It should be noted that income from real estate
wherever situated is exempt from taxation in the hands of
a resident of Massachusetts.   That is, Massachusetts legislators recognize that real estate wherever situated is certain
to be taxed on its value under the laws of the state in which
it lies, and they consequently refrain from imposing a
second tax.   But while income from real estate situated in
Connecticut or New York, for example, is accordingly exempt from taxation in the hands of residents of Massachusetts, under the Massachusetts income tax law, the income
from corporations organized in those states is not similarly
exempt.   The assumption on the part of Massachusetts is,
plainly, that such corporations are untaxed or are not taxed
to an extent corresponding to the burden of the tax imposed
upon Massachusetts corporations.   The assumption is probably not a correct one, at least as far as it concerns the taxation of corporations in the adjacent states which are most
important industrially.   Before the Massachusetts income
tax law was passed Connecticut had begun to tax the net
incomes of corporations at two per cent, a tax from which
the state derives a revenue of more than $2,000,000 a year.[1]
New York taxes corporations by means of a levy of four
and one-half per cent on net earnings, a tax which, together
with other corporation taxes of less importance fiscally,
yields over $30,000,000 annually.[2]

The actual effect of the Massachusetts legislation is to
discriminate against investment in foreign corporations on
the part of the residents of the state levying the income tax,
although investments in real estate outside Massachusetts
are not so discriminated against.   Even though the number

[1] Connecticut Tax Commissioner, *Report,* 1918, p. 52.
[2] New York State Comptroller, *Report,* 1921, p. xvii.

and amount of actual transfers of holdings from foreign
corporations to Massachusetts corporations which result
may be small, the unfortunate effects of such discrimination
upon interstate relations are not avoided. Furthermore,
the real purpose of the taxation of income from foreign
corporations paralleled by the exemption of Massachusetts
corporations has been very generally misunderstood by the
payer of the income tax in Massachusetts who has not followed the course of the law from the beginning. The impression has come to prevail far too generally in Massachusetts that the state adminstration is engaged in a consistent
attempt to force a change in security holding which will
benefit Massachusetts corporations, and even to suspect that
the corporations themselves are behind the provision.

The income tax laws of Wisconsin and New Mexico,
under which income derived from the securities of corporations which pay the state income tax is exempt from taxation as personal income, are slightly less discriminatory in
that they do not include provisions for the exemption of income from real estate. At the same time they do, however,
give ground for the popular misunderstanding which is
found in Massachusetts namely, that the taxing states in-
tend to force a withdrawal of funds from outside enterprises and reinvestment in domestic corporations.

An effort towards uniformity may take any one of three
directions. States which levy taxes on personal incomes
may continue to exempt income from sources already taxed
within the state, while imposing taxes on all other income,
in which case difficult questions of interstate relationships
as well as dissatisfaction on the part of the taxpapers who
are influenced to invest within the state of residence are
sure to result. Second, exemptions of income may be extended by carrying the plan of Massachusetts' exemption of
income from real estate wherever located to its logical con-

clusion, so that the result is the exemption of income the source of which is subject to any considerable amount of tax in any form and by any jurisdiction, a system which manifestly would be cumbersome, impracticable, and possibly entirely unworkable. The most practicable program is a simpler one. It rests upon the assumption that double taxation is harmful only when its burden is felt unequally by different individuals and different classes of taxpayers. With the universal operation of the federal income tax and the growing use of state taxes on personal incomes, double taxation is actually becoming increasingly prevalent. The only anxiety which need be felt is that the taxes should be fairly distributed. The taxation of corporate incomes by the federal government is accomplished together with the taxation of personal incomes without reference to the sources of those personal incomes. If the dates of taxation are carefully fixed, such a method probably accomplishes no appreciably unjust results. In the same way, the taxation by the individual states of all personal income, whether or not derived from corporate securities or from real estate, need arouse no opposition if the burden of taxation falls with uniformity upon taxpayers of equal ability. The state of affairs with regard to the taxation of corporations themselves is changing so rapidly that the legislators of any one state which is levying or contemplating the levy of a personal income tax need no longer assume that corporations in another state are not adequately taxed. Since that is true, interstate relations, the willingness of the taxpayer to contribute, and administrative efficiency may best be served by disregarding the source of the personal incomes of residents.

The taxation of the income of non-residents is quite another problem. The general trend of state personal income tax legislation seems to be in the direction of taxing

residents on their entire incomes and non-residents on that
part of their incomes derived within the state levying the
personal income tax.   From a general point of view the
result is a heavier rate of taxation upon persons of more
than moderate incomes whose sources of income transcend
state lines.   For example, a resident of Virginia who derives his income entirely from sources within that state is
taxed only once upon his income; but a resident of Virginia who renders professional services in New York
is taxed in Virginia upon all of his income and in New York
upon a part of it in addition.   In case the income is of any
considerable amount, the rates imposed are the maximum
rates of the mildly graduated scales in use in the two states,
and the income is subject to a higher rate of taxation than
it would have been in Virginia alone.   Under the present
terms of the Virginia law the taxpayer would be deprived
of credit from New York state for personal income taxes
paid in Virginia; for although New York grants a credit of
that kind in certain instances, it would deny it in this instance; for the credit is granted only in case the second
state grants a similar credit to residents of New York or
exempts from taxation the personal incomes of residents
of New York.

By its decisions in regard to the non-resident sections of
the Oklahoma and New York income tax laws the supreme
Court of the United States has established the *right* of the
states to tax the income of non-residents from sources
within the state levying the personal income tax, provided
that such non-residents are not discriminated against in the
matter of exemptions and deductions.   The question which
now remains is this: with the extension of the use of state
income taxes which seems probable with the next few
years, is the taxation of the incomes of non-residents likely
to bring about serious inequalities in the tax burden between

persons whose income-earning activities are confined to one
state and persons who earn income in two or more states?
If the levying of personal income taxes by the states should
become general, the question can only be answered in the
affirmative.   In such a case the imposition of a tax upon
the net income of *residents* only, as is now done in Massachusetts, would be the only way out of the difficulty; for
in that way every person would be taxed upon his entire
net income in his state of residence and no part of any
taxpayer's income would escape. As long as state income taxes are used by only a few states it will be possible
to continue the taxation of the incomes of non-residents,
but questions of law and justice may be expected to accumulate and increase in difficulty as long as such taxation is attempted.

4. *The new type of administration*

Owing in large part to the fact that administrative defects were held responsible for the failure of state income
tax laws before 1911, the organizations of the departments,
commissions, or bureaus which are charged with the assessment and collection of the personal income tax have been
built up anew in several of the states within the last few
years. The chief defect of the older systems was the
allotment of the work on the personal income tax to an
existing office, in most cases that of the state treasurer or
state auditor, with the expectation that the actual work of
assessment and collection would be done by the local assessors of property taxes.   This plan almost invariably proved
unsatisfactory. The local assessors found that the personal income tax was quite a different piece of tax legislation from any with which they had been accustomed to deal;
some of them objected to it on principle, believing the personal income tax to be a superfluous and unworkable sup-

erstructure on the system which they regarded as more reliable and trustworthy, that of the general property tax; and nearly all of them were accustomed to deal with a large amount of evasion of personal property taxes, and made ready for (and met) quite as much evasion of personal income taxes. Their new duties of collecting personal income taxes were added to heavy duties already undertaken in the assessment and collection of property taxes. The position of the supervisory officer was in too many cases somewhat similar, although the earlier income tax history furnishes several refreshing instances of state officials who labored with diligence and humor to overcome the inertia of their local representatives. Much of the opposition and criticism which was aimed at the Wisconsin income tax in its early days was actually caused, not by an opposition to the principle of the taxation of personal incomes by the states, but by a conviction that the administrative difficulties could never be overcome.

The innovation in administrative methods was probably the most important element in the Wisconsin income tax law of 1911. The state tax commission was given the administration of the tax, with power to divide the state into income tax districts and to appoint special assessors of incomes who should be subject to civil service requirements. The ordinary term of office was fixed at three years so that the local assessors might be given time in which to gain the good-will and respect of the communities in which their work was done.

Although the success of the Wisconsin plan was recognized almost from the beginning, it was several years before the same type of administration was adopted in another state. The Mississippi law of 1912 gave the administration into the hands of the state tax commission, but the regular local assessors had the assessment of income taxes in-

cluded with their duties.   The Mississippi income tax was
so badly planned from the beginning that its failure can
hardly be laid at the door of the local assessors, a fact
which the state tax commission has recognized in its frequent appeals for an entirely new income tax act.   In
Oklahoma the administration of the income tax law of
1915 was placed with the state auditor, with the assumption that the local work was to be done by the regular assessors.   The plan of administration adopted in Massachusetts
in 1916 shows the first real influence of the Wisconsin
method, and again in Massachusetts, as in Wisconsin, the
machinery of administration has been held in large part
responsible for the success of the income tax.   The state
tax commissioner was made the nominal head of the income
tax system, but it was suggested that he should appoint an
income tax deputy who should have the actual supervision
and control of the administration.   The state was divided
into income tax districts, with special assessors of income,
as in Wisconsin.   It is noteworthy that this second state to
adopt centralized administration was also the second state
to make a financial success of the law.

From the point of view of improvement in administrative
methods the history of the next few years is a repetition.
The states which followed the old plan (Missouri and Delaware with new laws and Virginia and North Carolina with
revisions) had only a moderate degree of success; while
New York, with a plan much like that of Wisconsin, found
the income tax a fruitful source of revenue.   In New York
the control was not given to the state tax commission, as
the framers of the original bill had urged, but, for political
reasons, to the state comptroller.   The type of administration provided for was so nearly similar to that which would
have been developed under the state tax commission that
little anxiety was felt lest the results of the tax should be

less satisfactory. A special income-tax bureau was formed as one of the bureaus of the state comptroller's department, and the state was divided into income tax districts with branch offices, as required by law.

The North Dakota plan of administration was also modelled on lines similar to those of Wisconsin, but on account of the various difficulties which the unusual form of the law has produced the actual effects of the type of administration itself have been almost lost sight of. New Mexico, which adopted a law which showed many traces of the more successful of the state laws which preceded it, was backward in this particular respect, and give the administration to the state treasurer without the provision of new local officials. The new law recommended for New Mexico by the special revenue commission which reported in 1920 would give the central control to an enlarged state tax commission.

The success of Wisconsin, Massachusetts, and New York with the personal income tax is now widely known. Among tax experts it is an almost universal opinion that the single most nearly indispensable condition of this success has been centralized and specialized administration. The recommendations of the Committee on Model Taxation and the terms of the model law drafted by that committee are similar to those of the New York law, with the exception of the fact that the committee on model taxation is in favor of having the tax administered by the state tax commission.

5. *Assessment, collection, and review*

The state income tax laws show an increasing tendency to follow the federal income tax law in requiring the return of income by the taxpayer, a process usuall termed " self assessment." The New York law requires the filing of returns similar to those made to the federal government, in the same month in which the federal returns are due, and accompanied by the amount of the tax due as computed on the face of the return.   In Massachusetts returns are required to be made early in the calendar year but the tax is subsequently assessed and collected through the office of the state tax commissioner, or, more accurately, through the income tax deputy.   In Wisconsin a third method is in use: returns are made by individuals to the local assessors of incomes and the taxes assessed are certified to the local assessors of property taxes.   These taxes appear on the local tax rolls but are separately entered as income taxes.   The income taxes are then paid at the same time and in the same manner as personal property taxes.   Among the other states which tax personal incomes the only example of a procedure like that of New York and the federal government is that specified in the New Mexico law of 1919.   In all of the other states the return of personal income by the taxpayer is required but the payment of the tax is made only after the tax has been assessed by designated officials.

In the states in which income taxes are paid at the same time and in the same manner as other taxes, it is argued that the taxpayers who do not have bank accounts and for whom the whole process of paying a personal income tax is a difficult and annoying one have the task facilitated by its combination with an old and familiar process, that of paying property taxes.   There has been no necessity for installing this system in Massachusetts and New York, for in those states in which the income tax rates are not applied to incomes below the exemption limits of the federal law all of the individuals liable to the state income tax are familiar with the process of making out income tax returns and of remitting to the federal authorities the amount of the tax due.   In Wisconsin, where individuals with incomes smal-

ler than those to which the federal rates apply are reached
by the state income tax, individuals who for the most part
are unfamiliar with ordinary banking procedure, the other
method of collection has probably averted many inaccura-
cies of payment.   It is probable that any state income taxes
which may be imposed in the near future will not be applied
to incomes below the federal exemption limits and it is
therefore to be expected that the federal procedure of collection at the time of self-assessment will be followed by
states which pass new laws for the taxation of personal incomes.

The extension of taxes on personal incomes and the elab-
oration of the rates of taxation to an unforeseen extent have
produced the necessity for making careful provision for appeal, review, and abatement of taxes wrongfully assessed.
Wisconsin has established county boards of review to deal
with complaints with regard to the assessment of income
and has designated the state tax commission as the body
to which appeal from the decisions of the county board of
review should be made.   In Massachusetts any person aggrieved by his assessment may appeal directly to the tax
commissioner, and may appeal from the decision of the tax
commissioner to a board of appeal, whose decision is final.
In New York the aggrieved taxpayer appeals directly to
the comptroller, and if dissatisfied with the comptroller's
decision he must appeal to the courts.

The method of applying directly to the tax commission
or commissioner for revision of the tax assessed against the
taxpayer, with the possibility of appeal to the courts if the
decision is unsatisfactory to the taxpayer, is endorsed by
the Committee on Model Taxation.   The principal objection
which may be raised against this method is the fact that
the courts are not usually in possession of all of the details
necessary for the fairest consideration of income tax mat-

ters to as great an extent as a board of appeal created for
the express purpose of dealing with disputed tax questions.
If the review is first made by the higher taxing officials,
however, it is probable that the important details of the
matter under dispute will have been adequately covered.
The Massachusetts law appears to provide for the most
equitable method of abatement of taxes assessed, but the
period covered by the operation of state income taxes is still
so short that no method has yet conclusively demonstrated
its superiority.

6. *An assessment roll for the income tax*

A subject which was not taken up by the model tax committee but which has been given a considerable amount of
space in the publications of the National Tax Association
is that of an assessment roll for the income tax.[1]   The use
of the assessment roll for this type of tax has been most
strongly urged by Professor Plehn, who regards it as one
of the indispensable conditions of efficient collection.
Ordinarily the process of assessment for a direct tax is
very formal in character.   With both federal and state income taxes the process has been conducted with scant
ceremony.   The lists which are made out are in most instances compiled *after* the income taxes are paid.   A great
deal of uncertainty as to the actual amounts of tax payable,
on the part of the collectors as well as on the part of the
taxpayers, is the result.   In Wisconsin, where the income
tax was introduced before the federal income tax was in
existence, some of the present difficulties were avoided,—

[1] C. C. Plehn, " An Assessment Roll for the Income Tax," *Bulletin
of the National Tax Association,* vol. v, no. 7 (April, 1920), pp. 231-
220; " Assessment of Income Tax, Once More," *Bulletin,* etc., vol. vi,
no. 6 (March, 1921), pp. 177-179; A. E. James, " An Assessment Roll
for the Income Tax," *Bulletin,* etc., vol. vi, no. 2 (Nov., 1920), pp. 47-51.

possibly because no other alternative but a formal roll suggested itself to those who drafted the income tax law. Income tax assessments were required to be entered on the regular local assessment rolls, but to be separately classified. The result has been a more formal procedure than that with which the federal income taxpayer or other state income taxpayers have become familiar.

Few tax experts are inclined to dwell as pointedly upon the disadvantages of the absence of an assessment roll for the income tax as is Professor Plehn. A recent comment is as follows:[1]

There is no good reason why the Wisconsin system should not work in the federal Government. If the question were a new one, no one would hesitate to choose between them. But the matter is a practical one vitally affected by the fact that in Wisconsin the state waits a year for the money, while under the federal system the money is paid in part with the return and all of it before the return is audited.

This comment is even more to the point when considered in connection with the matter of state collection, for in New York the whole amount of the tax due is remitted at the time when the personal return is submitted. The settlement of the taxpayer's exact liability before the tax is paid is undoubtedly an end which should be striven for, but in the generally confused condition of state income taxes at the present time the difficulties which follow from this lack are probably of minor significance.

7. *Collection and information at the source*

Collection (otherwise known as " stoppage " or " withholding ") at the source means withholding a certain amount of the sum otherwise due to individuals by the cor-

[1] James, *op. cit.*, p. 50.

porations or other agencies paying wages, salaries, dividends, or amounts due in any other form, to facilitate the payment of income taxes by those individuals. The system has been used extensively in connection with the payment of the income tax in Great Britain, where it is believed that the method of stoppage at the source is effective in preventing evasions of the income tax and in producing accurate declarations of income, for the reason that the amount deducted at the source is in many cases larger than the amount which should ultimately be paid, and in order to get the exemption, abatement, or relief due him the taxpayer must declare his income in detail. The system of stoppage at the source is so important in this connection that it has been repeatedly said in Great Britain that it is indispensable to the success of the income tax, and any provision, however minor in appearance, which is liable to disturb its operation in any way is attacked by the officials of the inland revenue system.

Collection at the source was attempted on a large scale in this country for income taxes due under the federal revenue law of 1916. Individuals, corporations, or other agencies paying wages, salaries, interest, rent, dividends, or other sums of the kind were required to withhold an amount corresponding to the normal tax and to remit that amount to the federal income tax officials. The plan proved to be extremely unpopular, largely, it is believed, on account of the delays in refunding to the taxpayers the amounts due as abatements. In the federal law of 1918 withholding at the source was limited to amounts paid to non-resident aliens, and a system of *information* at the source somewhat like the plan already in use in Massachusetts [1] was substituted. Every person, corporation, or other agency pay-

---

[1] *Laws of Massachusetts,* 1916, ch. 269, sec. 25.

ing another $1,000 or more in interest, rent, salaries, wages, premiums, annuities, compensation, remuneration, emoluments, or other fixed and determinable gains, profits and income must report such payments to the federal income tax authorities.   This type of information at the source is strongly objected to by certain critics, who regard it as productive of "moral degradation,"[1] but it probably produces less dissatisfaction than the original effort to collect the normal tax itself at the source.

In Wisconsin a partial requirement of information at the source was made in the provision that in order to be allowed to make deductions from income for wages paid corporation must furnish information concerning employees paid $700 or more a year.   The Massachusetts law passed in 1916 contained a more inclusive provision for information at the source: payments to all persons to whom more than $1,800 a year is paid in the previous calendar year must be reported, a provision which with minor changes is still in force.   No other state followed this plan until 1919, when the New York personal income tax law was so framed as to require information at the source for all persons to whom $1,000 or more was paid in a calendar year.   The New York law also included profisions for withholding at the source income for personal services of non-residents (salaries, wages, commissions, gratituties, emoluments, and perquisites).   In the law in its original form the rate at which these taxes were to be withheld failed to correspond to the rates for the final payment of the tax, and the legislature was forced to amend the law so that the amounts wihheld should correspond to the tax rates of one, two, and three per cent on the various classes of taxable income.

The only other attempt to collect personal income taxes

[1] C. C. Plehn, *Introduction to Public Finance* (4th ed., New York, 1920), p. 283.

at the source has been made by North Dakota. The law passed in that state in 1919 provided for collection at the source of all income taxes on dividends, interest, profits, premiums, and annuities. This provision proved to be difficult to administer, and it was repealed later in the same year.

As the laws stood at the beginning of 1921, collection at the source had failed everywhere in the United States except in New York, where it still remained to be adequately tested. This almost universal failure in this country presents a curious problem, for it was assumed at the time when both federal and state income tax laws were developing rapidly that collection at the source would prove as great a bulwark of income taxation and as great a protection against fraud and evasion as in Great Britain. It was even argued that collection at the source was peculiarly adaptable to the condition of affairs with regard to incomes in the United States, since corporate securities were widely held in this country and wages and salaries paid largely through corporations. Possibly the root of the trouble lies in the rapidity with which the status of the recipients of taxable income changes in this country, or possibly in the diifficulty with which individuals and corporations adapt themselves to administrative methods which involve " red tape." The objections which are heard most frequently have to do, not with the status of incomes or with the roundabout nature of the process, but simply with the unfairness of shifting the burden of the taxpaying process to the wrong shoulders. The Committee on Model Taxation does not advocate collection at the source, for the reasons that in its opinion such a method " presents serious administrative difficulties, imposes unwarranted burdens upon third parties in respect of transactions which strictly concern only the taxpayers and the government, and not infrequently tends to shift the

burden of the tax to the wrong shoulders." [1]   The committee does, however, advocate information at the source
" as is now done under the Massachusetts and Wisconsin
income taxes."   The experience of the state of New York
with collection at the source at a progressive rate for the
taxes of non-residents will illuminate the whole problem,
and, if successful, may yet influence other states to undertake it.

8. *The distribution of the proceeds of the income tax*

Only the three states which depend on the income tax
for large sums, Wisconsin, Massachusetts, and New York,
distribute the proceeds of the income tax direct to the
localities.   In two others, Delaware and New Mexico, the
proceeds of the tax are devoted largely to educational purposes and distributed according to the needs of the educational institutions.   The New Mexico law has been so delayed in its operation that Delaware furnishes the only
example of the practical details of the latter type of distribution.

The Wisconsin plan, by which 70 per cent of the proceeds
of the income tax goes to the local unit from which the
revenue was derived, 20 per cent to the county, and 10 per
cent to the state, has the advantage of great simplicity.
During the period of rapid industrial change which followed
the outbreak of the European War the surprising effects
of distribution according to as simple a scheme as this were
demonstrated.   Unexpectedly large amounts of revenue
were brought to localities which happened to have prosperous industrial concerns located within their borders but
which were accustomed to only the most modest of revenues
and which seemed unable to invent ways in which to make

[1] *Preliminary Report,* p. 17.

use of the amounts distributed to them by the state income tax offices.

New York has adopted an equally simple plan. The proceeds over and above the expenses of administration are divided equally between the state and the counties according to assessed valuation. The distribution in Massachusetts has been along different lines. When the law was first passed it was planned to distribute the proceeds of the income tax in such a way as to reimburse the local taxing units for the losses which they might be expected to meet through the abolition of the personal property tax and the substitution of a tax on intangibles as a part of the personal income tax. The amount to be paid to each city or town was to be " an amount equal to the difference between the amount of the tax levied upon personal property in such city or town in the year nineteen hundred and fifteen and the amount, computed by the tax commissioner, that would be produced by a tax on personal property actually assessed in such city or town for the year nineteen hundred and seventeen at the same rate of taxation as prevailed therein in the year nineteen hundred and fifteen." [1] Before the proceeds of the income tax were distributed the expenses of administration were to be subtracted. In 1919 a scheme was adopted for reducing by degrees the amounts paid to the local units as reimbursement for the losses through the removal of the personal property taxes, to expire after its completion in 1927, after which date the amount to be distributed and paid to the cities and towns was to be determined in proportion to the amount of the state tax imposed upon each of them in each year. [2] A little later in 1919 another change was made, and a scheme of reimbursement in relation

[1] *Laws of 1916*, ch. 269, sec. 23.
[2] *Laws of 1919*, ch. 314.

to the needs of the schools was adopted.[1] The plan included
the payment of lump sums to teachers and other educational
officials of various grades of salary, and supplementary
reimbursements for those cities and towns in which the
assessed valuation was below a certain ratio to the school
attendance. This plan was opposed on the same grounds on
which such a plan of expenditure is usually opposed in any
locality,—namely, for the reason that it forces the urban
districts to pay for the schools of the poorer and rural districts, but it was carried through.

The plan used in Delaware results in the distribution of
the proceeds of the income tax to the various school districts on the basis of enrollment.

The distribution of the yield of state income taxes is
one of the most important problems connected with the
utilization of that form of taxation. The interest in the
development of the income tax principle itself has been so
great that this part of the question has been too much
neglected, with the result that the purposes to which the
product of the tax may be devoted have not been adequately safeguarded. The amusing excess of local income in certain places in Wisconsin during the recent industrial changes has already been noted. In New York,
where the distributi n to the localities is made according to assessed valuation, the results are "weird and mean-
ingless" according to A. E. Holcomb, secretary of the
National Tax Association.[2] In states in which the tax
has been unexpectedly productive and in which no safe-
guards whatever have been put around the disposition of
the proceeds of the tax there has undoubtedly been a temp-

[1] *Laws of 1919*, ch. 363.

[2] A. E. Holcomb, " State Income Taxes," *Bulletin of the National Tax
Association*, vol. vi, no. 4 (Jan., 1921), p. 126.

tation to use the funds for purposes which are not immediately urgent.

Mr. Holcomb holds that a distribution for educational purposes is superior to the methods used in Wisconsin and New York:[1]

A method of distribution, at once reasonable and having the added advantage of popularity and attractiveness to the general public seems to us to be educational purposes. This is so because of the preponderating amount of that expense, as compared with other governmental expenses. It would readily absorb the yield of the income tax, without a suggestion of " surplus ". A measure for such distribution is available in the school enrollment, and finally, and most important, the definite reflection in each tax bill of a sharp reduction in the largest item, would have a marked effect in the attitude of the taxpayer towards the tax.

The same results could in large measure be obtained by assigning the yield to the state educational department, to be distributed under its supervision as so-called " state aid." . . . .

The distribution of a large part of the proceeds of the income tax to the local units in some way is desirable under present conditions. The income tax is intended as a substitute for the unsatisfactory personal property tax in nearly all of the states in which it has recently been adopted or enlarged in scope, and as such a reimbursement is due to the local taxing units for those sums which, if they did not actually receive, they should have received under the old system. The Committee on Model Taxation regards this question of distribution as one to which a dogmatic answer cannot be given, since the local units are relieved from a part of their tax burden in either case,—that is, they are assisted if the revenue is distributed directly to them, but they are also assisted if the proceeds of the income tax are assigned to the state treasury and are used for general

[1] Holcomb, *op. cit.*, p, 127.

state purposes, for the direct state tax is correspondingly lightened.   This is undeniably true, but in this matter, as in many other instances, the actual reliefs or burdens conferred through the operation of taxes are extremely likely to be assumed by the least intelligent of the taxpayers to remain where they first fall.   Hence a better understanding on the part of the average taxpayer of the actual effect of the income tax is obtained if at least a part of the proceeds is distributed to the local unit in which the taxpayer resides.   Furthermore, the distribution should be made with such a purpose and in such a way that the taxpayer is made conscious of the lightening of his tax burden.   The effect of the actual process of this distribution was in fact felt clearly and with excellent effect upon the popular sentiment towards the income tax when at the close of 1920 the New York state comptroller made the refunds due the localities under the state income tax law.   The method which the Committee on Model Taxation suggests in its preliminary report, that of a division of the proceeds of the income tax in the proportions which the state and local expenditures bear to the total state and local expenditure combined, is probably a workable and satisfactory one.   If, further, this method is combined with one by which the details of distribution are worked out according to some educational factor, as is advised by Mr. Holcomb, the results should be more satisfactory than those now obtained in Wisconsin or New York.

9. *Financial results*

The productivity of the state income tax under modern conditions can be no more vividly described than by the citation of New York's $37,000,000 in receipts from the operation of the tax on individual incomes in the first year of collection.   When the scale of incomes and of the state

budget is taken into consideration the financial results in
Wisconsin and Massachusetts are hardly less impressive.
It has been demonstrated that it is possible for a state to
collect one-fifth as much as the federal government collects
by means of the income tax, to reap a sum which is almost
equal to one-third of the state's revenue, and to conduct the
operations of assessment and collection at a cost of
(approximately) two per cent on assessments,—the record
of Massachusetts with the income tax. These facts are
significant in any forward look over the financial affairs of
the American states. The income tax is not now regarded
as a cure-all for financial ills; it is recognized that it cannot
properly occupy a position of sole importance in the
taxing plan of a state, but must be fitted into a diversified
tax scheme; but the question of its productiveness and
economy is now answered, and in that respect the judgment
of the nineteenth century has been reversed.

10. *Conclusion*

In concluding a study of the income tax in modern industrial countries in 1911, Professor Seligman emphasized
three lessons which might be learned from the history of
the income tax: first, the income tax was coming, in the
United states as elsewhere; second, the tax worked better
from year to year and from decade to decade; and, third, its
success depended, almost more than in the case of any
other modern institution, upon administrative machinery.
A survey of the ten years of tax history which have passed
since those words were written brings added proof of each
of the three statements, for state income taxes in particular
as well as for taxes of wider application. State income
taxes are coming,—pushed to the front by the ever-increasing dissatisfaction with general property taxes, by the lure
of a large yield, and by the willingness to experiment which

the financial changes of the war have brought about. From year to year improvements have been made and the tax has worked more effectively,—as Massachusetts has adapted and improved the income tax devices of Wisconsin and as New York has seized upon both, utilized them, and moved a step ahead. Finally, the realization of the prime importance of workable administrative machinery is now nation-wide. Under the financial conditions of the present the modern income tax must be regarded as one of the most productive and one of the most satisfactory sources of state revenue.

APPENDIX I

EXTRACT FROM THE "PRELIMINARY REPORT OF THE COMMITTEE APPOINTED
BY THE NATIONAL TAX ASSOCIATION TO PREPARE A PLAN OF A
MODEL SYSTEM OF STATE AND LOCAL TAXATION,"
SEPTEMBER, 1918

III. THE PROPOSED PERSONAL INCOME TAX

Section 11. The first decision reached by the committee was that in the proposed model system of state and local taxation there should be a personal tax levied with the exclusive view of carrying out the principle that every person having taxable ability should pay a direct tax to the government under which he is domiciled. There appeared to be four forms of personal taxation which have been employed for this purpose.

The first of these is the poll tax. It is evident, however, from the nature of the case that this tax would be utterly inadequate to accomplish the object in view, even if levied at graduated rates, as has sometimes been done in other countries. It would be so unequal and so far inferior to the other forms of personal taxation that it cannot be deemed worthy of serious consideration. Whether, as a supplement to an adequate system of personal taxation, it might be desirable to retain the poll tax as a means of insuring some contribution from people owning no property and having small incomes, the committee preferred not to consider in this report. It has been our desire to confine ourselves to main issues, and not to undertake to solve every minor problem of taxation. We, therefore, say nothing about the poll tax, except that it is inadequate for the purpose that we have in view, and cannot be recommended as an important element in any system of state and local taxation.

The second method of imposing the personal tax would be to levy a tax upon every man's net fortune, that is, upon the total of his assets in excess of his liabilities, without exemption of any kind of asset or exclusion of any liability. This would not mean a general property tax, but a net property tax such as is found in some countries in Europe. It would be a tax levied not upon property as such, but upon net fortune as a measure of the citizen's personal liability to contribute to the government under which he is domiciled. It would be entirely distinct from any tax that might be levied objectively upon property, as property, at the place of its situs, and would have to be levied exclusively upon the property owner at his place of domicile. It would necessarily be levied at a moderate rate, perhaps $3 per $1000, which would correspond approximately to a six per cent income tax upon investments yielding five per cent. Although precedents may be found in other countries for such a personal tax levied upon net fortunes, the committee has concluded that it is not to be recommended for adoption in the United States. Such a tax would raise the difficult constitutional question of the right of a state to levy a tax even upon the *net* fortune of a citizen if that fortune included tangible property located in another commonwealth. It is, furthermore, foreign to American experience, and would certainly not lead us along the line of least resistance. Since the coming of the federal income tax, it is obvious that it is easier for the states, and more convenient for the taxpayers, to adopt income rather than net fortune as the measure of the obligation of the citizen to contribute to the government under which he lives.

The third method of personal taxation is what may be called a presumptive income tax, that is, a tax levied upon persons according to certain external indicia which are taken to be satisfactory measures of taxable ability. House rent is the index commonly used in such presumptive income taxes, and a tax on rentals has been proposed in times past by special commissions in Massachusetts and New York. Such a tax would be comparatively easy to administer, and would raise no difficult constitutional questions. It would undoubtedly be better than an income tax or a tax on net fortunes if those taxes were badly administered. But the amount that a citizen pays for house rent is after all such a very imperfect and inadequate indication of his income or fortune that the committee is unwilling to recommend it to any state in which there is any reasonable expectation that conditions are, or may presently become, favorable for the introduction of a better form of personal tax. It appears that in France, where the tax on rentals has been in continuous operation since the Revolution, there is so little correspondence between house rents and taxable ability that in the greater part of the communes the taxing officials disregard to a greater or less extent the letter of the law, and assess people according to what they appear able to pay. The committee finds, therefore, that the tax on rentals is not to be recommended except, perhaps, as a last resort in states where administrative and other conditions are unfavorable to the introduction of any better form of personal taxation.

There remains a fourth form of personal taxation, the personal income tax. By this is meant a tax levied upon persons with respect to their incomes which are taxed not objectively as incomes but as elements determining the taxable ability of the persons who receive them. This tax is better fitted than any other to carry out the principle that every person having taxable ability shall make a reasonable contribution to the support of the government under which he lives. It is as fair in principle as any tax can be; under proper conditions, it can be well administered by an American state, as Wisconsin and Massachusetts have proved; it is a form of taxation which meets with popular favor at the present time, and therefore seems to offer the line of least resistance. The committee, therefore, is of the opinion that a personal income tax is the best method of enforcing the personal obligation of the citizen for the support of the government under which he lives, and recommends it as a constituent part of a model system of state and local taxation.

Section 12. While it is impossible in this report to describe the proposed taxes in every detail, it is essential that the

committee should explain at least in broad outlines the manner
in which these taxes should be levied. In so doing it will be
necessary to refer constantly to the general principles previously stated, and to adjust the details of each tax in such a
manner as to enable it to carry into effect logically and consistently the principle upon which it is based.

Since the purpose of the personal income tax is to enforce
the obligation of every citizen to the government under which
he is domiciled, it is obvious that this tax must be levied only
upon persons and in the states where they are domiciled. It
is contrary to the theory of the tax that it should apply to the
income from any business as such, or apply to the income of
any property as such. The tax should be levied upon persons
in respect of their entire net incomes, and should be collected
only from persons and at places where they are domiciled. It
should not be collected from business concerns, either incorporated or unincorporated, since such action would defeat the
very purpose of the tax.

At first thought this proposal will doubtless seem objectionable to many, who will ask why a state should not tax all incomes derived from business or property located within its
jurisdiction, irrespective of whether the recipients are residents or non-residents. And if the personal income tax were
the only one proposed, the objection would be well grounded.
The committee, however, is under the necessity of reconcil-
ing the conflicting claims of the states, and of doing so in a
manner that will avoid unjust double and triple taxation of
interstate business and investments. We, therefore, propose
as the only practicable remedy a system which comprises three
taxes, each of which is designed to satisfy fully and fairly
the legitimate claims of our several states. We are elsewhere
providing methods by which property will be taxed where located and business will be taxed where it is carried on. At this
point, we are dealing exclusively with a personal tax designed
to enforce the right of our states to tax all persons domiciled
within their jurisdictions; and we are merely insisting that,
in enforcing this claim, the states shall act consistently, and

shall confine personal taxation to persons and attempt to levy
it only at the place of domicile. If the personal income tax
is levied in any other way, it will simply reproduce and perpetuate the old evil of unjust double taxation of interstate
property and interstate business.

The second detailed recommendation we have to make is
that the personal income tax shall be levied in respect of the
citizen's entire net income from all sources. Under existing
constitutional limitations, of course, interest upon the bonds
of the United States and the salaries of federal officials cannot
be taxed by the states, but we recommend that all other sources
of income be subject to the income tax without exception or
qualification. We are aware that, under the unreasonable and
unworkable requirements of the general property tax, it has
appeared desirable in times past to exempt state and local
bonds from taxation, to exempt real-estate mortgages, and to
grant various other exemptions. All such exemptions are inconsistent with the theory of the tax we here propose, and
should be discontinued as rapidly as the circumstances of each
case permit. Against the policy which led to these exemptions
under the general property tax we here offer no criticism. But
we are now dealing with a tax which is designed to be a part of
a new system of taxation, and it is evident that none of the
considerations which led to the exemptions created under the
general property tax are applicable to a personal income tax
levied upon the principle we here advocate. The personal obligation of the citizen to contribute to the support of the government under which he lives should not be affected by the form
his investments take, and to exempt any form of investment can
only bring about an unequal, and therefore an unjust distribution of this tax. Our reasoning applies, of course, to the
exemption which agencies of the·federal government now enjoy. But that is a matter which is beyond the control of the
states, and for the purposes of this report it will be considered
a fixed datum which must be accepted.[1]

[1] We here follow the view that has long prevailed concerning existing

Our third specific recommendation is that the personal income tax should be levied upon net income defined substantially as a good accountant would determine it. We submit no formal definition at this time, and content ourselves with referring to the provisions of the Wisconsin and the Massachusetts income taxes. Our recommendation means that operating expenses and interest on indebtedness must be deducted, but we wish to call attention to the fact that the issue by the federal government of large amounts of bonds which are exempt from local taxation will make it necessary for the states to limit the interest deduction to an amount proportional to the income which the taxpayer derives from taxable sources. This would mean that if a person derives half of his income from taxable sources and one-half from tax-exempt federal bonds, he should be permitted to deduct but one-half of the interest that he pays upon his indebtedness. Any other procedure will tend to make the personal income tax a farce in many cases and will give occasion for legitimate complaint.

The fourth recommendation relates to the exemption of small incomes. The committee believes that the amount of income exempted from the personal income tax should not exceed $600 for a single person and $1200 for a husband and wife, with a further exemption of $200 for each dependent up to a number not to exceed three. This would give us a maximum exemption of $1,800 for a family consisting of husband, wife, and three children or other dependents. We recognize, however, that conditions may well differ in various states, and have decided to make no specific recommendations about the amount of the exemptions granted to persons having small incomes. We limit ourselves to the above statement of the maximum exemptions that should be granted and the further observation

restrictions on the taxing power of the states. In two recent cases (Peck *v.* Lowe and U. S. Glue Co. *v.* Oak Creek, 247 U. S.) the court has developed a doctrine which may justify the belief that a net income tax, levied upon state officials along with all other persons, with respect to their entire net incomes, might not be held to be a tax upon agencies of the federal government, and therefore forbidden by federal decisions.

that, under a democratic form of government, it is desirable
to exempt as few people as possible from the necessity of
making a direct personal contribution toward support of
the state.[1]

Our fifth recommendation is that the rate of the income tax
shall be the same for all kinds of income, that is, that it shall
not be differentiated according to the sources from which
income is derived. If the tax stood by itself, a strong argument could be made for imposing a higher rate upon funded
than upon unfunded incomes. But the tax is, in fact, designed
to be part of a system of taxation in which there will be a tax
upon tangible property. Under this system there will be heavier
taxation of the sources from which funded incomes are derived; and there will, therefore, be little if any ground for
attempting to differentiate the rates of the personal income
tax. Such differentiation, furthermore, would greatly compli-
cate the administration of the tax, and would lead to numerous
difficulties. Upon all accounts, therefore, we recommend that
there shall be no differentiation of the rate.

In the sixth place we recommend that the rates of taxation
shall be progressive, the progression depending upon the amount
of the taxpayer's net income. Concerning the precise schedule
of rates, we offer certain general recommendations. The
lowest rate should not be less than one per cent, and under
present conditions we regard it as inexpedient for any state to
impose a rate higher than six per cent. The classes of taxable
income to which the various rates apply need not be smaller
than $1000, and probably should not be larger. It results from
what has been said that if the exemption to a single person be
placed at $600, we would recommend a tax of one per cent upon
any amount of income between $600 and $1600; a tax of two
per cent upon any amount of income betweeen $1600 and
$2600; a tax of three per cent upon any amount of income

---

[1] For administrative convenience we recommend that, in order to
minimize the number of very small tax bills, no person liable to pay an
income tax shall be assessed for less than $1.00.

between $2600 and $3600; a tax of four per cent upon any amount of income between $3600 and $4600; a tax of five per cent upon any amount of income between $4600 and $5600; and a tax of six per cent upon all income in excess of $5600. We present these figures merely for the purpose of illustrating our preferences, and make no definite recommendation except that the rates of the personal income tax should be moderate, and should be, as nearly as practicable, uniform throughout the United States.

Our seventh suggestion concerns the administration of the proposed tax. No argument can be needed by the National Tax Association to support our recommendation that the administration of the personal income tax should be placed in the hands of state officials. This we regard as an indispensable condition for the successful operation of any state income tax, and we should be disinclined to recommend the adoption of an income tax by any commonwealth that is unwilling to turn over its administration to a well organized and properly equipped state tax department. Local administration of an income tax has never worked well, and in our opinion, never can operate satisfactorily. It is obvious, finally, that a state tax commission, or commissioner, is the proper agent to administer the proposed tax; and we desire to record our belief that satisfactory results are hardly to be expected if the administration is turned over to any other state officials. Upon this whole question of administration, which is of the most vital importance, we are fortunate in being able to rely upon the authority of the opinions repeatedly expressed by the conferences of the National Tax Association. We are glad also to point to the experience of Wisconsin and Massachusetts.

Our eighth recommendation is that the personal income tax be collected from taxpayers, upon the basis of strictly enforced and controlled returns, and without any attempt to collect it at the source. Upon this point there might have been doubt several years ago. But the experience of Wisconsin and Massachusetts shows conclusively that, with good administration, a reasonable tax upon incomes can be collected in the manner we have recommended, with the general cooperation of the taxpayers and with the minimum amount of evasion. Collection at source presents serious administrative difficulties, imposes unwarranted burdens upon third parties in respect of transactions which strictly concern only the taxpayers and the government, and not infrequently tends to shift the burden of the tax to the wrong shoulders. What we seek is a personal income tax which shall not be shifted and shall bring home to the taxpayer, in the most direct possible form, his personal obligation for the support of the government under which he lives. Collection at the source is plainly inconsistent with the purpose of such a tax. We recommend, however, that in certain cases information at the source be required as is now done under the Massachusetts and Wisconsin income taxes. Such information is helpful to the administrative officials, and does not alter the incidence or otherwise affect injuriously the operation of a personal income tax.

Section 13. The only remaining point is that of the proper disposition of the proceeds of this tax. So far as our general plan of taxation is concerned, it is immaterial whether the revenue from the personal income tax is retained in the state treasury, distributed to the local political units, or divided between the state and local governments. It is probable, furthermore, that the same solution may not be advisable in every state. If the state should keep the entire revenue, then every section of the state would benefit to the extent that such revenue might reduce the direct state tax. Upon the other hand, if the revenue from the income tax is distributed wholly to the local units, as is now the case in Massachusetts, the lightening of local burdens tends to reduce the pressure of the direct state tax. It seems probable that in most cases a division of the revenue would be considered preferable; and in such cases we suggest that the state governments might well retain a proportion corresponding to the proportion which state expenditures bear to the total of the state and local expenditures, and that the same principle should apply in determining the share received by each of the subordinate political units.

Thus in case state expenditures amount to one-fifth of the total, county expenditures to two-fifths, and municipal expenditures to two-fifths, the state should receive one-fifth of the revenue from the income tax, the counties two-fifths, and the municipalities two-fifths. Whether distribution to the local units should be made upon the basis of the amount of the tax collected in each unit, or whether the tax should be distributed upon some other basis, is also immaterial to our general plan of taxation. In states where domiciliary changes occurring under the general property tax have not produced an unnatural concentration of wealth in certain localities, it will probably be best to distribute the revenue according to the domicile of the taxpayers. But where, as in Massachusetts, under the operation of the general property tax, wealth has been greatly concentrated in a few localities, such a method of distribution is obviously impossible and some other method must be found. In such a case, the income tax revenue might be utilized for a state school fund, or might be distributed among the localities according to the proportions in which they are required to contribute to the direct state tax. Since this entire question of distribution must be so largely affected by local conditions, the committee prefers to do no more than to offer these general suggestions.

APPENDIX II

DRAFT OF A PERSONAL INCOME TAX ACT

PREPARED FOR THE NATIONAL TAX ASSOCIATION BY THE COMMITTEE
APPOINTED TO PREPARE A PLAN FOR A MODEL SYSTEM OF STATE
AND LOCAL TAXATION. JANUARY, 1921

PERSONAL INCOME TAX

AN ACT PROVIDING FOR THE LEVYING, COLLECTING AND PAYING
OF AN INCOME TAX ON INDIVIDUALS

Be it Enacted by the Legislature of the State of ————

ARTICLE I

SHORT TITLE AND DEFINITIONS

Section 1. **Short title.** This Act shall be known and may be cited as The Personal Income Tax Act of 192—.

Sec. 2. **Definitions.** For the purposes of this act and unless otherwise required by the context:

1. The words " tax commission " mean the state tax commission.

2. The word " taxpayer " includes any individual or fiduciary subject to the tax imposed by this act.

3. The word " individual " means a natural person.

4. The word " fiduciary " means a guardian, trustee, executor, administrator, receiver, conservator, or any person, whether individual or corporate, acting in any fiduciary capacity for any person, estate or trust.

5. The word " person " includes individuals, fiduciaries, partnerships and corporations.

6. The word " corporation " includes joint-stock companies or associations and insurance companies.

7. The words "tax year" mean the calendar year in which the tax is payable.

8. The words "income year" mean the calendar year or the fiscal year, upon the basis of which the net income is computed under this act; if no fiscal year has been established they mean the calendar year.

9. The words "fiscal year" mean an income year, ending on the last day of any month other than December.

10. The word "paid" for the purposes of the deductions under this act, means "paid or accrued" or "paid or incurred", and the words "paid or accrued", "paid or incurred" and "incurred" shall be construed according to the method of accounting upon the basis of which the net income is computed under this act. The word "received" for the purpose of the computation of the net income under this act means "received or accrued", and the words "received or accrued" shall be construed according to the method of accounting upon the basis of which the net income is computed under this act.

11. The word "resident" applies only to individuals and includes for the purpose of determining liability to the tax imposed by this act, with reference to the income of any income year, any individual who shall be a resident of the state on April 15 of the tax year.

12. The words "foreign country" mean any jurisdiction other than one embraced within the United States. The words "United States", when used in a geographical sense, include the states, the territories of Alaska and Hawaii, the District of Columbia and the possessions of the United States.

ARTICLE II

IMPOSITION OF TAX

Sec. 200. **Individuals.** 1. A tax is hereby imposed upon every resident of the state, which tax shall be levied, collected and paid annually, with respect to his entire net income as herein, computed at the following rates, after deducting the exemptions provided in this act:

On the first $1000 of net income or any part thereof, one per cent;

On the second $1000 of net income or any part thereof, two per cent;

On the third $1000 of net income or any part thereof, three per cent;

On the fourth $1000 of net income or any part thereof, four per cent;

On the fifth $1000 of net income or any part thereof, five per cent;

On all net income in excess of $5000, six per cent.

2. Such tax shall first be levied, collected and paid in the year 1921 and with respect to the net income received during the calendar dear 1920 or during any income year ending during the twelve months ending March 31, 1921.

Sec. 201. **Fiduciaries.** 1. The tax imposed by this act shall be imposed upon resident fiduciaries, which tax shall be levied, collected and paid annually with respect to:

(a) That part of the net income of estates or trusts which has not been distributed or become distributable to beneficiaries during the income year. In the case of two or more joint fiduciaries, part of whom are non-residents of the state, such part of the net income shall be treated as if each fiduciary had received an equal share;

(b) The net income received during the income year by deceased individuals who, at the time of death were residents and who have died on or after April 15 of the tax year without having made a return;

(c) The entire net income of resident insolvent or incompetent individuals, whether or not any portion thereof is held for the future use of the beneficiaries, where the fiduciary has complete charge of such net income.

2. The tax imposed upon a fiduciary by this act shall be a charge against the estate or trust.

Article III

COMPUTATION OF TAX

Sec. 300. **Net income defined.** The words " net income " means the gross income of a taxpayer less the deductions allowed by this act.

Sec. 301. **Gross income defined.** 1. The words " gross income " includes gains, profits and income derived from salaries, wages, or compensation for personal service, of whatever kind and in whatever form paid, or from professions, vocations, trades, business, commerce, or sales, or dealings in property, whether real or personal, growing out of the ownership or use of or interest in such property; also from interest, rent, dividends, securities, or the transaction of any business carried on for gain or profit, or gains or profits and income derived from any source whatever. The amount of all such items shall be included in the gross income of the income year in which received by the taypayer, unless, under the methods of accounting permitted under this act, any such amounts are to be properly accounted for as of a different period.

2. The words " gross income," does not include the following items, which shall be exempt from taxation under this act:

(a) The proceeds of life-insurance policies and contracts paid upon the death of the insured to individual beneficiaries or to the estate of the insured;

(b) The amount received by the insured as a return of premium or premiums paid by him under life insurance, endowment or annuity contracts, either during the term or at the maturity of the term mentioned in the contract or upon surrender of the contract;

(c) The value of property acquired by gift, bequest, devise or descent (but the income from such property shall be included in gross income);

(d) Interest upon the obligations of the United States or its possessions;

(e) Salaries, wages and other compensation received from the United States by officials or employees thereof, including persons in the military or naval forces of the United States;

(f) Any amounts received through accident or health insurance or under workmen's compensation acts, as compensation for personal injuries or sickness, plus the amount of any damages received, whether by suit or agreement, on account of such injuries or sickness.

Sec. 302. **Basis of return of net income.** 1. Taxpayers who customarily estimate their income on a basis other than that of actual cash receipts and disbursements may, with the approval of the tax commission, return their net income under this act upon a similar basis. Taxpayers who customarily estimate their income on the basis of an established fiscal year instead of on that of the calendar year, may, with the approval of the tax commission, and subject to such rules and regulations as it may establish, return their net income under this act on the basis of such fiscal year, in lieu of that of the calendar year.

2. A taxpayer may, with the approval of the tax commission and under such regulations as it may prescribe, change his income year from fiscal year to calendar year or otherwise, in which case his net income shall be computed upon the basis of such new income year.

3. An individual carrying on business in partnership shall be liable for income tax only in his individual capacity and shall include in his gross income the distributive share of the net income of the partnership received by him or distributable to him during the income year.

4. Every individual, taxable under this act, who is a beneficiary of an estate or trust, shall include in his gross income the distributive share of the net income of the estate or trust, received by him or distributable to him during the income year. Unless otherwise provided in the law, the will, the deed or other instrument creating the estate, trust or fiduciary relation, the net income shall be deemed to be distributed or distributable to the beneficiaries (including the fiduciary as a beneficiary, in the case of income accumulated for future distribution) ratably, in proportion to their respective interests.

Sec. 303. **Determination of gain or loss.** For the purpose of ascertaining the gain or loss from the sale or other disposition of property, real, personal or mixed, the basis shall be, in the case of property acquired before January 1, ——, the fair market price or value of such property as of that date, if such price or value exceeds the original cost, and in all other cases, the cost thereof; *Provided*, that in the case of property which was included in the last preceding annual inventory used in determining net income in a return under this act, such inventory value shall be taken in lieu of cost or market value. The final distribution to the taxpayer of the assets of a corporation shall be treated as a sale of the stock or securities of the corporation owned by him and the gain or loss shall be computed accordingly.

Sec. 304. **Exchanges of property.** 1. When property is exchanged for other property, the property received in exchange shall, for the purpose of determining gain or loss, be treated as the equivalent of cash to the amount of its fair market value, provided a market exists in which all the property so received can be disposed of at the time of exchange, for a reasonably certain and definite price in cash; otherwise such exchange shall be considered as a conversion of assets from one form to another, from which no gain or loss shall be deemed to arise.

2. In the case of the organization of a corporation, the stock or securities received shall be considered to take the place of property transferred therefor and no gain or loss shall be deemed to arise therefrom.

3. When, in connection with the reorganization, merger or consolidation of a corporation, a taxpayer receives, in place of stock or securities owned by him, new stock or securities, the basis of computing the gain or loss if any shall be, in case the stock or securities owned were acquired before January 1, ——, the fair market price or value thereof as of that date, if such price or value exceeds the original cost, and in all other cases the cost thereof.

Sec. 305. **Inventory.** Whenever in the opinion of the tax commission the use of inventories is necessary in order clearly to determine the income of any taxpayer, inventories shall be taken by such taxpayer, upon such basis as the tax commission may prescribe, conforming as nearly as may be to the best accounting practice in the trade or business and most clearly reflecting the income, and conforming so far as may be, to the forms and methods prescribed by the United States Commissioner of Internal Revenue, under the acts of Congress then providing for the taxation of incomes.

Sec. 306. **Deductions.** In computing net income there shall be allowed as deductions:

(a) All the ordinary and necessary expenses paid during the income year in carrying on any trade or business, including a reasonable allowance for salaries or other compensation for personal services actually rendered, and including rentals or other payments required to be made as a condition to the continued use or possession, for the purposes of the trade or business, of property to which the taxpayer has not taken or is not taking title or in which he has no equity;

(b) All interest paid during the income year on indebtedness;

(c) Taxes paid or accrued within the income year, imposed by the authority of the United States or of any of its possessions or of any state, territory or the District of Columbia or of any foreign country; except inheritance taxes, and except income taxes imposed by this act and taxes assessed for local benefits, of a kind tending to increase the value of the property assessed;

(d) Losses sustained during the income year and not compensated for by insurance or otherwise, if incurred in trade or business;

(e) Losses sustained during the income year and not compensated for by insurance or otherwise, if incurred in any transaction entered into for profit, though not connected with the trade or business;

(f) Losses sustained during the income year, of property not connected with the trade or business, if arising from fires, storms, shipwreck or other casualty, or from theft, and not compensated for by insurance or otherwise;

(g) Debts ascertained to be worthless and charged off within the income year, if the amount has previously been included in gross income in a return under this act;

(h) A reasonable allowance for the depreciation and obsolescence of property used in the trade or business; and, in the case of mines, oil and gas wells, other natural deposits, and timber, a reasonable allowance for depletion; *Provided,* That in computing the deductions allowed under this paragraph, the basis shall be the cost (including in the case of mines, oil and gas wells and other natural deposits, the cost of development, not otherwise deducted), and in the case of property acquired prior to January 1, ——, the fair market value of the property (or the taxpayer's interest therein) on that date shall be taken in lieu of cost up to that date. The reasonable allowances under this paragraph shall be made under rules and regulations to be prescribed by the tax commission. In the case of leases the deductions allowed may be equitably apportioned between the lessor and lessee;

(i) In the case of taxpayers who keep regular books of account, upon an accrual basis and in accordance with standard accounting practice, reserve for bad debts and for contingent liabilities, under such rules and restrictions as the tax commission may impose. If the tax commission shall at any time deem the reserve excessive in amount, it may restore such excess to income, either in a subsequent year or as a part of the income of the income year and assess it accordingly.

Sec. 307. **Items not deductible.** In computing net income no deduction shall in any case be allowed in respect of:

(a) Personal, living or family expenses;

(b) Any amount paid out for new buildings or for permanent improvements or betterments, made to increase the value of any property or estate;

(c) Any amount expended in restoring property for which an allowance is or has been made;

(d) Premiums paid on any life-insurance policy covering the life of any officer or employee or of any individual financially interested in any trade or business carried on by the taxpayer, when the taxpayer is directly or indirectly a beneficiary under such policy.

Sec. 308. **Exemptions.** 1. There shall be deducted from the net income the following exemptions:

(a) In the case of a single individual, a personal exemption of $1000;

(b) In the case of the head of a family, or a married individual living with husband or wife, a personal exemption of $2000. A husband and wife living together shall receive but one personal exemption of $2000 against their aggregate net income; and in case they make separate returns, the personal exemption of $2000 may be taken by either or divided between them;

(c) $200 for each individual (other than husband and wife) dependent upon and receiving his chief support from the taxpayer, if such dependent individual is under eighteen years of age or is incapable of self-support, because mentally or physically defective;

(d) In the case of a fiduciary; if taxable under clause (a) of paragraph 1 of section 201, a personal exemption of $1000; if taxable under clause (b) of said paragraph, the same exemption as would be allowed the deceased, if living; if taxable under clause (c) of said paragraph, the same exemptions to which the beneficiary would be entitled.

2. The status on the last day of the income year shall determine the right to the exemptions provided in this section; *Provided* that a taxpayer shall be entitled to such exemptions for husband or wife or dependent who has died during the income year.

ARTICLE IV

RETURNS

Sec. 400. **Individual returns.** 1. Every resident, having a net income during the income year of $1000 or over, if single, or if married and not living with husband or wife; or having a net income for the income year of $2000 or over, if married and living with husband or wife; shall make a return under oath, stating specifically the items of his gross income and the deductions and exemptions allowed by this act.

2. If a husband and wife living together have an aggregate net income of $2000 or over, each shall make such a return, unless the income of each is included in a single joint return.

3. If the taxpayer is unable to make his own return, the return shall be made by a duly authorized agent or by a guardian or other person charged with the care of the person or property of such taxpayer.

Sec. 401. **Fiduciary returns.** 1. Every fiduciary subject to taxation under the provisions of this act, as provided in section 201 hereof, shall make a return under oath, for the individual, estate, or trust for whom or for which he acts, if the net income thereof amounts to $1000 or over.

2. The return made by a fiduciary shall state specifically the items of gross income, and the deductions and exemptions allowed by this act and such other facts as the tax commission may prescribe. Under such regulations as the tax commission may prescribe, a return may be made by one of two or more joint fiduciaries.

3. Fiduciaries required to make returns under this act shall be subject to all the provisions of this act which apply to individuals.

Sec. 402. **Information at source.** 1. Every individual, partnership, corporation, joint stock company or association or insurance company, being a resident or having a place of business in this state, in whatever capacity acting, including lessees or mortgagors of real or personal property, fiduciaries, employers and all officers and employees of the state or of any political subdivision of the state, having the control, receipt, custody, disposal or payment of interest (other than interest coupons payable to bearer), rent, salaries, wages, premiums, annuities, compensations, remunerations, emoluments or other fixed or determinable annual or periodical gains, profits and income, amounting to $1000 or over, paid or payable during any year to any taxpayer, shall make complete return thereof under oath, to the tax commission, under such regulations and in such form and manner and to such extent as may be prescribed by it.

2. Every partnership, having a place of business in the state, shall make a return, stating specifically the items of its gross income and the deductions allowed by this act, and shall include in the return the names and addresses of the individuals who would be entitled to share in the net income if distributed, and the amount of the distributive share of each individual. The return shall be sworn to by any one of the partners.

3. Every fiduciary shall make, under oath, a return for the individual, estate or trust for whom or for which he acts, if the net income thereof, distributed or distributable to beneficiaries during the year is $1000 or over, in which case the fiduciary shall set forth in such return the items of the gross income, the deductions allowed by this act, the net income, the names and addresses of the beneficiaries, the amounts distributed or distributable to each and the amount, if any, lawfully retained by him for future distribution. Such return may be made by one of two or more joint fiduciaries.

Sec. 403. **Time and place of filing returns.** Returns shall be in such form as the tax commission may from time to time prescribe and shall be filed with the tax commission, at its main office or at any branch office which it may establish, on or before the fifteenth day of the fourth month next after the preceding calendar year or any income year ending after such calendar year and on or before the thirty-first day of March. In case of sickness, absence or other disability, or whenever in its judgment good cause exists, the tax commission may allow further time for filing returns. There shall be annexed to the return the affidavit or affirmation of the taxpayer making the return, to the effect that the statements contained therein are true. The tax commission shall cause to be prepared blank forms for the said returns and shall cause them to be distributed throughout the state and to be furnished upon application, but failure to receive or secure the form shall not relieve any taxpayer from the obligation of making any return herein required.

Sec. 404. **Failure to file returns; supplementary returns.** If the tax commission shall be of the opinion that any taxpayer has failed to file a return, or to include in a return filed, either intentionally or through error, items of taxable income, it may require from such taxpayer a return, or a supplementary return, under oath, in such form as it shall prescribe, of all the items of income which the taxpayer received during the year for which the return is made, whether or not taxable under the provisions of this act. If from a supplementary return, or otherwise, the tax commission finds that any items of income, taxable under this act, have been omitted from the original return it may require the items so omitted to be disclosed to it, under oath of the taxpayer, and to be added to the original return. Such supplementary return and the correction of the original return shall not relieve the taxpayer from any of the penalties to which he may be liable under any provision of this act. The tax commission may proceed under the provisions of section 502 of this act whether or not it requires a return or a supplementary return under this section.

ARTICLE V

COLLECTION AND ENFORCEMENT OF TAX

Sec. 500. **Time and place of payment of tax.** 1. The full amount of the tax payable, as the same shall appear from the face of the return, shall be paid to the tax commission at the office where the return is filed, at the time fixed by law for filing the return. If the time for filing the return shall be extended, interest at the rate of 6 per cent per annum, from the time when the return was originally required to be filed, to the time of payment, shall be added and paid.

2. The tax may be paid with uncertified check, during such time and under such regulations as the tax commission shall prescribe, but if a check so received is not paid by the bank on which it is drawn, the taxpayer by whom such check is tendered shall remain liable for the payment of the tax and for all legal penalties, the same as if such check had not been tendered.

Sec. 501. **Examination of returns.** 1. As soon as practicable after the return is filed, the tax commission shall examine it and compute the tax, and the amount so computed by the tax commission shall be the tax. If the tax found due shall be greater than the amount theretofore paid, the excess shall be paid to the tax commission within ten days after notice of the amount shall be mailed by the tax commission.

2. If the return is made in good faith and the understatement of the tax is not due to any fault of the taxpayer, there shall be no penalty or additional tax added because of such understatement, but interest shall be added to the amount of the deficiency at the rate of 1 per cent for each month or fraction of a month.

3. If the understatement is due to negligence on the part of the taxpayer, but without intent to defraud, there shall be added to the amount of the deficiency 5 per cent thereof, and in addition, interest at the rate of 1 per cent per month or fraction of a month.

4. If the understatement is false or fraudulent, with intent to evade the tax, the tax on the additional income discovered to be taxable shall be doubled and an additional 1 per cent per month or fraction of a month shall be added.

5. The interest provided for in this section shall in all cases be computed from the date the tax was originally due to the date of payment.

6. If the amount of tax found due as computed shall be less than the amount theretofore paid, the excess shall be refunded by the tax commission out of the proceeds of the tax retained by it as provided in this act.

Sec. 502. **Additional taxes.** If the tax commission discovers from the examination of the return or otherwise that the income of any taxpayer, or any portion thereof, has not been assessed, it may, at any time within two years after the time when the return was due, assess the same and give notice to the taxpayer of such assessment, and such taxpayer shall thereupon have an opportunity, within thirty days, to confer with the tax commission as to the proposed assessment. The limitation of two years to the assessment of such tax or additional tax shall not apply to the assessment of additional taxes upon fraudulent returns. After the expiration of thirty days from such notification the tax commission shall assess the income of such taxpayer or any portion thereeof which it believes has not theretofore been assessed and shall give notice to the taxpayer so assessed, of the amount of the tax and interest and penalties if any, and the amount thereof shall be due and payable within ten days from the date of such notice. The provisions of this act with respect to revision and appeal shall apply to a tax so assessed. No additional tax amounting to less than one dollar shall be assessed.

Sec. 503. **Warrant for the collection of taxes.** If any tax imposed by this act or any portion of such tax be not paid within sixty days after the same becomes due, the tax commission shall issue a warrant under its hand and official seal directed to the sheriff of any county of the state, commanding him to levy upon and sell the real and personal property of the taxpayer, found within his county, for the payment of the amount thereof, with the added penalties, interest and the cost of executing the warrant and to return such warrant to the tax commission and pay to it the money collected by virtue thereof by a time to be therein specified, not less than sixty days from the date of the warrant. The sheriff shall within five days after the receipt of the warrant, file with the clerk of his county a copy thereof, and thereupon the clerk shall enter in the judgment docket, in the column for judgment debtors, the name of the taxpayer mentioned in the warrant, and in appropriate columns the amount of the tax or portion thereof and penalties for which the warrant is issued and the date when such copy is filed, and thereupon the amount of such warrant so docketed shall become a lien upon the title to and interest in real property or chattels real of the taxpayer against whom it is issued in the same manner as a judgment duly docketed in the office of such clerk. The said sheriff shall thereupon proceed upon the same in all respects, with like effect, and in the same manner prescribed by law in respect to executions issued against property upon judgments of a court of record, and shall be entitled to the same fees for his services in executing the warrant, to be collected in the same manner. If a warrant be returned not satisfied in full, the tax commission shall have the same remedies to enforce the claim for taxes against the taxpayer as if the people of the state had recovered judgment against the taxpayer for the amount of the tax.

Sec. 504. **Tax a debt.** Every tax imposed by this act, and all increases, interest and penalties thereon, shall become, from the time it is due and payable, a personal debt, from the person or persons liable to pay the same, to the state of ———.

Sec. 505. **Action for recovery of taxes.** Action may be brought at any time by the attorney general of the state, at the instance of the tax commission, in the name of the state, to recover the amount of any taxes, penalties and interest due under this act.

Sec. 506. **Tax upon settlement of fiduciary's account.** 1. No final account of a fiduciary shall be allowed by the probate court unless such account shows, and the judge of said court finds, that all taxes imposed by the provisions of this act upon said fiduciary, which have become payable, have been paid, and that all taxes which may become due are secured by bond, deposit or otherwise. The certificate of the tax commission and the receipt for the amount of the tax therein certified shall be conclusive as to the payment of the tax, to the extent of said certificate.

2. For the purpose of facilitating the settlement and distribution of estates held by fiduciaries, the tax commission, with the approval of the attorney general, may, on behalf of the state agree upon the amount of taxes at any time due or to become due from such fiduciaries under the provisions of this act, and payment in accordance with such agreement shall be full satisfaction of the taxes to which the agreement relates.

Article VI

PENALTIES

Sec. 600. **Penalties.** 1. If any taxpayer, without intent to evade any tax imposed by this act shall fail to file a return of income or pay a tax, if one is due, at the time required by or under the provisions of this act, but shall voluntarily file a correct return of income and pay the tax due within sixty days thereafter, there shall be added to the tax an additional amount equal to five per cent thereof, but such additional amount shall in no case be less than one dollar and an additional one per cent for each month or fraction of a month during which the tax remains unpaid.

2. If any taxpayer fails voluntarily to file a return of income or to pay a tax if one is due within sixty days of the time required by or under the provisions of this act, the tax shall be doubled, and such doubled tax shall be increased by one per cent for each month or fraction of a month from the time the tax was originally due to the date of payment.

3. The tax commission shall have power, upon making a record of its reasons therefor, to waive or reduce any of the additional taxes or interest provided in subdivisions 1 and 2 of this section or in subdivisions 2, 3 and 4 of section 501.

4. If any taxpayer fails to file a return within sixty days of the time prescribed by this act, any judge of the —————— court, upon petition of the tax commission, or any ten taxable residents of the state, shall issue a writ of mandamus requiring such person to file a return. The order of notice upon the petition shall be returnable not later than ten days after the filing of the petition. The petition shall be heard and determined on the return day or on such day thereafter as the court shall fix, having regard to the speediest possible determination of the case, consistent with the rights of the parties. The judgment shall include costs in favor of the prevailing party. All writs and processes may be issued from the clerk's office in any county and, except as aforesaid, shall be returnable as the court shall order.

5. Any person who, without fraudulent intent, fails to pay any tax or to make, render, sign or verify any return, or to supply any information, within the time required by or under the provisions of this act, shall be liable to a penalty of not more than $1000, to be recovered by the attorney general, in the

name of the people, by action in any court of competent jurisdistion.

6. Any person or any officer or employee of any corporation, or member or employee of any partnership, who, with intent to evade any requirement of this act or any lawful requirement of the tax commission thereunder, shall fail to pay any tax or to make, sign or verify any return or to supply any information required by or under the provisions of this act, or who, with like intent, shall make, render, sign or verify any false or fraudulent return or statement, or shall supply any false or fraudulent information, shall be liable to a penalty of not more than $1000, to be recovered by the attorney general in the name of the people, by action in any court of competent jurisdiction, and shall also be guilty of a misdemeanor and shall, upon conviction, be fined not to exceed $1000 or be imprisoned not to exceed one year, or both, at the discretion of the court.

7. The attorney general shall have the power, with the consent of the tax commission, to compromise any penalty for which he is authorized to bring action under subdivisions 5 and 6 of this section. The penalties provided by such subdivisions shall be additional to all other penalties in this act provided.

8. The failure to do any act required by or under the provisions of this act shall be deemed an act committed in part at the office of the tax commission in ————. The certificate of the tax commission to the effect that a tax has not been paid, that a return has not been filed or that information has not been supplied, as required by or under the provisions of this act, shall be prima-facie evidence that such tax has not been paid, that such return has not been filed or that such information has not been supplied.

9. If any taxpayer, who has failed to file a return or has filed an incorrect or insufficient return and has been notified by the tax commission of his delinquency, refuses or neglects within twenty days after such notice to file a proper return, or files a fraudulent return, the tax commission shall determine the income of such taxpayer according to its best information

and belief and assess the same at not more than double the
amount so determined. The tax commission may in its discretion allow further time for the filing of a return in such case.

ARTICLE VII

REVISION AND APPEAL

Sec. 700. **Revision by tax commission.** A taxpayer may
apply to the tax commission for revision of the tax assessed
against him, at any time within one year from the time of the
filing of the return or from the date of the notice of the assessment of any additional tax. The tax commission shall grant
a hearing thereon and if, upon such hearing, it shall determine
that the tax is excessive or incorrect, it shall resettle the same
according to the law and the facts and adjust the computation
of tax accordingly. The tax commission shall notify the
taxpayer of its determination and shall refund to the taxpayer
the amount, if any, paid in excess of the tax found by it to be
due. If the taxpayer has failed, without good cause, to file
a return within the time prescribed by law, or has filed a
fraudulent return or, having filed an incorrect return, has failed,
after notice, to file a proper return, the tax commission shall
not reduce the tax below double the amount for which the taxpayer is found to be properly assessed.

Sec. 701. **Appeal.** The determination of the tax commission upon any application made by a taxpayer for revision of
any tax, may be reviewed in any court of competent jurisdiction by a complaint filed by the taxpayer against the tax
commission in the county in which the taxpayer resides or has
his principal place of business, within thirty days after notice
by the tax commission of its determination, given as provided
in section 700 of this act. Thereupon, appropriate proceedings
shall be had and the relief, if any, to which the taxpayer may
be found entitled may be granted and any taxes, interest or
penalties paid, found by the court to be in excess of those
legally assessed, shall be ordered refunded to the taxpayer,
with interest from time of payment.

Article VIII

ADMINISTRATION

Sec. 800. Tax commission to administer this act; districts. The tax commission shall administer and enforce the tax herein imposed, for which purpose it may divide the state into districts, in each of which a branch office of the tax commission may be established. It may from time to time change the limits of such districts.

Sec. 801. Powers of tax commission. The tax commission, for the purpose of ascertaining the correctness of any return or for the purpose of making an estimate of the taxable income of any taxpayer, shall have power to examine or cause to be examined by any agent or representative designated by it for that purpose, any books, papers, records or memoranda, bearing upon the matters required to be included in the return, and may require the attendance of the taxpayer or of any other person having knowledge in the premises, and may take testimony and require proof material for its information, with power to administer oath to such person or persons.

Sec. 802. Officers, agents and employees. 1. The tax commission may appoint and remove a person to be known as the income tax director who, under its direction shall have supervision and control of the assessment and collection of the income taxes provided in this act; the tax commission may also appoint such other officers, agents, deputies, clerks and employees as it may deem necessary, such persons to have such duties and powers as the tax commission may from time to time prescribe.

2. The salaries of all officers, agents and employees employed by the tax commission shall be such as it may prescribe, not to exceed such amounts as may be appropriated therefor by the legislature, and the members of the tax commission and such officers, agents and employees shall be allowed such reasonable and necessary traveling and other expenses as may be incurred in the performance of their duties, not to exceed the amounts appropriated therefor by the legislature.

3. The tax commission may require such of the officers, agents and employees as it may designate, to give bond for the faithful performance of their duties in such sum and with such sureties as it may determine, and all premiums on such bonds shall be paid by the tax commission out of monies appropriated for the purpose of this act.

Sec. 803. **Oaths and acknowledgments.** The members of the tax commission and such officers, as it may designate, shall have the power to administer an oath to any person or to take the acknowledgment of any person in respect of any return or report required by this act or the rules and regulations of the tax commission.

Sec. 804. **Publication of statistics.** The tax commission shall prepare and publish annually statistics reasonably available, with respect to the operation of this act, including amounts collected, classifications of taxpayers, income and exemptions, and such other facts as are deemed pertinent and valuable.

Sec. 805. **Secrecy required of officials; penalty for violation.** 1. Except in accordance with proper judicial order or as otherwise provided by law, it shall be unlawful for the members of the tax commission, any deputy, agent, clerk or other officer or employee, to divulge or make known in any manner the amount of income or any particulars set forth or disclosed in any report or return required under this act. Nothing herein shall be construed to prohibit the publication of statistics, so classified as to prevent the identification of particular reports or returns and the items thereof, or the inspection by the attorney general or other legal representatives of the state, of the report or return of any taxpayer who shall bring action to set aside or review the tax based thereon, or against whom an action or proceeding has been instituted to recover any tax or any penalty imposed by this act. Reports and returns shall be preserved for three years and thereafter, until the tax commission orders them to be destroyed.

2. Any offense against subdivision one of this section shall be punished by a fine of not exceeding one thousand dollars or by imprisonment not exceeding one year, or both, at the

discretion of the court, and if the offender be an officer or employee of the state, he shall be dismissed from office and be incapable of holding any public office in this state for a period of five years thereafter.

3. Notwithstanding the provisions of this section, the tax commission may permit the commissioner of internal revenue of the United States, or the proper officer of any state imposing an income tax upon the incomes of individuals, or the authorized representative of either such officer, to inspect the income tax returns of any individual, or may furnish to such officer or his authorized representative an abstract of the return of income of any taxpayer or supply him with information concerning any item of income contained in any return, or disclosed by the report of any investigation of the income or return of income of any taxpayer; but such permission shall be granted or such information furnished to such officer or his representative, only if the statutes of the United States or of such other state, as the case may be, grant substantially similar privileges to the proper officer of this state charged with the administration of the personal income tax law thereof.

Sec. 806. **Regulations.** The tax commission may from time to time make such rules and regulations, not inconsistent with this act, as it may deem necessary to enforce its provisions.

ARTICLE IX

MISCELLANEOUS

Sec. 900. **Distribution of the income tax.**

[Provision should be made whereby the proper officials shall be notified concerning the amount each locality is to receive from the income tax, in time to enable them to take account of such receipts when determining the amount of the local tax levied in each year.

Care should be taken to provide that a reasonable amount be withheld from distribution to the state or to the localities, in order to enable the commission to promptly make refunds to which taxpayers are found to be entitled.

For purposes of reference, the following methods of distribution contained in the statutes of various states having income tax laws, may be useful:

Delaware, L. 1917, Ch. 8; 1919, Ch. 157, Art. 14, § 212.

Mass., L. 1917, Ch. 209, 317, 339; 1918, Ch. 107, 154, 219; 1919, Ch. 314, § 1; Ch. 363, Part I.

N. Y., L. 1920, Ch. 694.

Wisc., L. 1917, Ch. 485.]

Sec. 901. **Exemption of intangible personal property from taxation.**

[Provision should be made for exempting intangible personal property from taxation under the property tax, as recommended in the Preliminary Report of the committee. The wording of such a provision will necessarily have to depend upon the language employed in the tax law of each state, and no provision can possibly be drawn which will be applicable to all states. The importance of providing for such exemption is so great that the committee feels obliged to record here its belief that a personal income tax cannot be expected to operate satisfactorily in a state which continues to tax intangible personal property under the property tax.

For purposes of reference, the following exemption provisions, contained in the statutes of various states having income tax laws, may be useful:

Mass., L. 1918, Ch. 257, § 69.

N. Y., L. 1920, Ch. 120.

No. Dak., L. 1919, Spec. Sess., Ch. 62.

Wis., L. 1911, Ch. 658, Secs. 2 & 3 (p. 999).]

Sec. 902. **Contract to assume tax illegal.** It shall be unlawful for any person to agree or contract directly or indirectly to pay or assume or bear the burden of any tax payable by any taxpayer under the provisions of this act. Any such contract or agreement shall be null and void and shall not be enforced or given effect by any court.

Sec. 903. **Unconstitutionality or invalidity.** If any clause, sentence, paragraph, or part of this act shall, for any reason, be adjudged by any court of competent jurisdiction to

be invalid, such judgment shall not affect, impair, or invalidate
the remainder of this act, but shall be confined in its operation
to the clause, sentence, paragraph or part thereof directly involved in the controversy in which such judgment shall have
been rendered. No caption of any section or set of sections
shall in any way affect the interpretation of this act or any
part thereof.

Sec. 904. **Taking effect of the act.** This act shall take
effect on ————.

[Since several months are required for the work preliminary
to the assessment of an income tax, the date at which the law
becomes effective ought to be such as to leave sufficient time
for such work.]

BIBLIOGRAPHY

GENERAL WORKS

Adams, H. C., *Science of Finance* (New York, 1899).
Black, H. C., *Treatise on the Law of Income Taxation* (Kansas City, 1915).
Ely, R. T., *Taxation in American States and Cities* (New York, 1888).
Kennan, K. K., *Income Taxation* (Milwaukee, 1910).
Kinsman, D. O., *The Income Tax in the Commonwealths of the United States* (New York, 1903).
Montgomery, R. H., *Income Tax Procedure* (New York, 1920).
Plehn, C. C., *Introduction to Public Finance* (4th ed., New York, 1920).
Seligman, E. R. A., *The Income Tax* (Revised ed., New York, 1914).
Seligman, E. R. A., *Progressive Taxation in Theory and Practice* (Revised ed., New York, 1918).
Wells, D. A., *Theory and Practice of Taxation* (New York, 1900).

OFFICIAL REPORTS

California:
   Commission on Revenue and Taxation, *Report*, 1906.
Connecticut:
   Tax Commissioner, *Biennial Report*, 1918.
Delaware:
   State Treasurer, *Reports*, 1917, 1919.
Georgia:
   Special Revenue Commission, *Report*, 1920.
Massachusetts:
   Commission appointed to inquire into the Expediency of Revising and Amending the Laws of the Commonwealth relating to Taxation, *Report*, 1897.
   Joint Special Committee on Taxation, *Report*, 1919..
   Tax Commissioner, *Reports*, 1917-1921.
Mississippi:
   Senate and House Committee to Consider the State's Revenue System and Fiscal Affairs, *Report*, 1918.
   Tax Commission, *Reports*, 1917, 1919.

New Mexico:
  Special Revenue Commission, *Report*, 1920.
  Tax Commission, *Report*, 1920.
New York:
  Comptroller, *Report*, 1920.
  Joint Legislative Committee, *Report*, 1916.
  Special Joint Committee on Taxation and Retrenchment, *Report*, 1921.
  State Tax Commission, *Reports*, 1918, 1919,
North Carolina:
  State Tax Commission, *Report*, 1919.
  State Treasurer, *Report*, 1920.
North Dakota:
  Tax Commissioner, *Report*, 1920.
Ohio:
  Special Joint Taxation Committee, *Report*, 1919.
Oklahoma:
  State Auditor, *Report*, 1912.
South Carolina:
  Joint Special Committee on Revenue and Taxation, *Report*, 1921.
  Tax Commission, *Reports*, 1915, 1917.
United States:
  Bureau of the Census, *Financial Statistics of States*, 1918, 1919.
  Internal Revenue, *Statistics of Income*, 1917, 1918.
Virginia:
  Auditor of Public Accounts, *Reports*, 1917, 1918.
Wisconsin:
  State Tax Commission, *Reports*, 1912-1920.
  Treasurer, *Report*, 1918.

SIGNED ARTICLES

Adams, T. S., "The Significance of the Wisconsin Income Tax," *Political Science Quarterly*, vol. xxviii, no. 4 (Dec. 1913).
Adams, T. S., "The Wisconsin Income Tax," *American Economic Review*, vol. i, no. 4 (Dec. 1911).
Bullock, C. J., "Operation of the Massachusetts Income Tax Law," *Quarterly Journal of Economics*, vol. xxxii, no. 3 (May, 1918).
Bullock, C. J., "Taxation of Property and Income in Massachusetts," *Quarterly Journal of Economics*, vol. xxxi, no. 1 (Nov. 1916).
Kennan, K. K., "The Wisconsin Income Tax," *Annals of the American Academy of Political and Social Science*, vol. lviii (1915).
Kinsman, D. O., "The Present Period of Income Tax Activity in the American States, *Quarterly Journal of Economics*, vol. xxiii, no. 2 (Feb. 1909).

Lutz, H. L., " The Progress of State Income Taxation since 1911," *American Economic Review,* vol. x, no. 1 (March, 1920).

Lyons, T. E., " The Wisconsin Income Tax," *Annals of the American Academy of Political and Social Science,* vol. lviii (1915).

Plehn, C. C. " An Assessment Roll for the Income Tax," *Journal of Political Economy,* vol. xxvii, no. 10 (Dec. 1919).

Seligman, E. R. A., " The New York Income-Tax," *Political Science Quarterly,* vol. xxxiv, no. 4 (Dec. 1919).

Seligman, E. R. A., " Are Stock Dividends Income," *American Economic Review,* vol. ix, no. 3 (Sept. 1919).

Shelton, W. A., " The Income Tax in Georgia," *Journal of Political Economy,* vol. xviii, no. 8 (Oct. 1910).

Sydenstricker, E., " A Brief History of Taxation in Virginia," *Legislative Reference Bureau of Virginia,* 1915.

PROCEEDINGS AND BULLETINS

Bulletin of the National Tax Association (New York).

Proceedings of the National Tax Association (1918-1921).

Proceedings of the New York State Conference on Taxation (1919).

INDEX